# A Supplementary Catalog of Wind Band and Wind Ensemble Repertoire

## Books by David Whitwell

*Philosophic Foundations of Education*
*Foundations of Music Education*
*Music Education of the Future*
*The Sousa Oral History Project*
*The Art of Musical Conducting*
*The Longy Club: 1900–1917*
*A Concise History of the Wind Band*
*Wagner on Bands*
*Berlioz on Bands*
*Chopin: A Self-Portrait*
*La Téléphonie and the Universal Musical Language*
*Extraordinary Women*
*Aesthetics of Music in Ancient Civilizations*
*Aesthetics of Music in the Middle Ages*
*Aesthetics of Music in the Early Renaissance*

## The History and Literature of the Wind Band and Wind Ensemble Series

*Volume 1 The Wind Band and Wind Ensemble Before 1500*
*Volume 2 The Renaissance Wind Band and Wind Ensemble*
*Volume 3 The Baroque Wind Band and Wind Ensemble*
*Volume 4 The Wind Band and Wind Ensemble of the Classical Period (1750–1800)*
*Volume 5 The Nineteenth-Century Wind Band and Wind Ensemble*
*Volume 6 A Catalog of Multi-Part Repertoire for Wind Instruments or for Undesignated Instrumentation before 1600*
*Volume 7 Baroque Wind Band and Wind Ensemble Repertoire*
*Volume 8 Classical Period Wind Band and Wind Ensemble Repertoire*
*Volume 9 Nineteenth-Century Wind Band and Wind Ensemble Repertoire*
*Volume 10 A Supplementary Catalog of Wind Band and Wind Ensemble Repertoire*
*Volume 11 A Catalog of Wind Repertoire before the Twentieth Century for One to Five Players*
*Volume 12 A Second Supplementary Catalog of Early Wind Band and Wind Ensemble Repertoire*
*Volume 13 Name Index, Volumes 1–12, The History and Literature of the Wind Band and Wind Ensemble*

www.whitwellbooks.com

*David Whitwell*

# A Supplementary Catalog of Wind Band and Wind Ensemble Repertoire

## THE HISTORY AND LITERATURE OF THE WIND BAND AND WIND ENSEMBLE, VOLUME 10

EDITED BY CRAIG DABELSTEIN

WHITWELL PUBLISHING • AUSTIN, TEXAS, USA

Whitwell Publishing, Austin 78701
www.whitwellbooks.com

Printed in the United States of America

PAPERBACK
ISBN-13: 978-1-936512-49-2
ISBN-10: 1936512491

All images used in this book are in the public domain except where otherwise noted.

Composed in Bembo Book

# Contents

# Foreword

*The History and Literature of the Wind Band and Wind Ensemble*

This volume, Number 10, is a supplement to the catalog of the original manuscripts and early prints associated with the wind band and contained in Volumes 6 to 9 of this series. The compositions listed in this volume represent the author's continued research in European libraries, particularly during several visits to Italy and England, during the years 1982 to 1990.

As in the case of the earlier volumes, the content is limited to compositions which date before the year 1900 and all spellings are given as they are found in the original materials.

David Whitwell
Austin, Texas

# Instrumentation Code

As an abbreviation for wind instrumentation I use a code of 0000-0000, representing:
flute, oboe, clarinet, bassoon - trumpet, horn, trombone, tuba.

Thus:

| | |
|---|---|
| 3000- | means a work for three flutes |
| -204 | means a work for two trumpets and four trombones |
| 1-1; 2 cornetts | means bassoon, trumpet, and two cornetts. |

# Text Abbreviations

| | |
|---|---|
| MS | Manuscript |
| EP | Early Print |
| MP | Modern Print (after 1900) |

# Secondary Sources

In addition to my own research in European libraries, some material has been included from the following sources, which are identified in the text with the author's name acknowledged in brackets.

| | |
|---|---|
| Anesa | Marino Anesa, *Musicia in Piazza*, Bergamo, 1988. |
| Lamnon | Douglas C. Lanroon, "Music for Wind Ensembles from the Oettingern-Wallerstein Music Collection," in the *NACWPI Journal*, Winter, 1988-1989. |
| Rietz | Julius Rietz, *Felix Mendelssohn Bartholdy*, from 1833 to 1847 [1864] |

# Library Abbreviations for this Catalog

Where the location of a work is known, the library is given in abbreviation according to the following international RISM system. Shelf-marks, or call-numbers, are given immediately after the library and are contained by (parentheses).

In the interval since this catalog was first published in 1990 there has been a reunification of Germany with the result that the old RISM library symbols have been changed and indeed in many cases the music has been moved to the Staatsbibliothek in Berlin. In this catalog, however, we retain the old RISM symbols and shelf-mark because even in those cases where the music has been moved to a new location the old information is necessary for the new library to identify these specific manuscripts for those who may want copies today.

## BRD: West Germany (Bundesrepublik Deutschland)

| | |
|---|---|
| HR | Harburg, Fürstlich Ottingen-Wallerstein'sche Bibliothek, Schloss Harburg |
| HRD Fü | Herdringen, Bibliothek, Fürstenberg-Herdringen |
| KA | Karlsruhe, Badische Landesbibliothek, Musikabteilung |
| Sl | Stuttgart, Württembergische Landesbibliothek |

## DDR: East Germany (Deutsche Demokratische Republik)

| | |
|---|---|
| Bds | Berlin, Deutsche Staatsbibliothek, Musikabteillmg |

## GB: Great Britain

| | |
|---|---|
| GB:Lbm | London, The British Museum |

## I: Italy

| | |
|---|---|
| ACRz | Biblioteca Comunale Zelantea (formerly: Acireale) |
| Ad | Biblioteca San Rufino Cattedrale, Assisi |
| Adria | Archivio del duomo, Assisi |
| AGN | Biblioteca Emidiana, Chiesa Parrocchiale di S. Emidio (Agnone) |
| AN | Ancona, Biblioteca Comunale, "Benincasa" |
| Bc | Civico Museo Bibliografico Musicale, Bologna |
| Bsf | San Francesco Convento Biblioteca, Bologna |
| BAR | Biblioteca Comunale Sabino Loffredo, Teatro Comunale G. Curci, Barletta |

| | |
|---|---|
| BGc | Biblioteca Civica Angelo Mai, Bergamo |
| BGi | Civico Istituto Musicale Gaetano Donizetti, Bergamo |
| BRc | Brescia, Biblioteca Conservatorio (Istituto Musicale Venturi) |
| BZtoggenburg | Conte Toggenburg (private library), Bolzano |
| CDO | Codogno, Biblioteca civica popolare, "L. Ricca" |
| Chiogga | Filippini Biblioteca |
| CMGd | Casalmaggiore (Cremona), Archivio del Duomo |
| Colambaro | Biblioteca privata Barcello |
| COR | Biblioteca Comunale, Correggio |
| CR | Biblioteca Governativa e Biblioteca Civica, Sala di Musicologia Gaetano Cesari, Cremona |
| CR | Biblioteca Statale, Cremona |
| CRg | Biblioteca Governativa e Civica, Cremona |
| CRE | Biblioteca Comunale, Crema |
| FAN | Biblioteca Comunale Federiciana, Fano |
| Fa | Firenze, Archivio dell 'Annunziata |
| Fc | Conservatorio di Musica Luigi Cherubini, Firenze |
| FEM | Biblioteca Comunale, Finale Emilia |
| FZac | Archivio Capitolare, Faenza |
| Gandino | Archivio Parrocchiale |
| Gl | Conservatorio di Musica Nicolo Paganini, Genova |
| JESI | Comunale Biblioteca, Jesi |
| Leffe | Raccolta privata Pezzoli, Leffe |
| Ls | Biblioteca Seminario Vescovile, Lucca |
| LU | Biblioteca Comunale Fabrizio Trisi, Lugo |
| MAC | Biblioteca Comunale Mozzi-Borgetti, Macerata |
| Ma | Milano, Biblioteca Ambrosiana |
| Mc | Conservatorio di Musica Giuseppe Verdi, Milano |
| Mr | Ricordi (Casa Editrice) , Milano |
| Mscala | Biblioteca Teatrale Liva Simoni, Museo Teatrale alIa Scala, Milano |
| Messina | Universitaria Biblioteca Universitaria, Messina |
| MOe | Biblioteca Estense e Universitaria, Modena |
| MOl | Modena, Liceo Musicale "Vecchi" |
| Nc | Conservatorio di Musica San Sebastiano, Napoli |
| Nf | Biblioteca Oratoriana dei Gerolamini, Napoli |
| NOd | Biblioteca Capitolare del Duomo, Novara |
| NOVg | Novara, Archivio di San Gaudenzio |
| OS | Biblioteca Musicale Greggiati, Ostiglia |
| PAas | Archdivio di Stato, Pama |
| PCd | Duomo, Biblioteca e Archivio Capitolare, Piacenza |
| Pi(l) | Padova, Istituto Musicale "Pollini" (Biblioteca del Liceo Musicale) |

| | |
|---|---|
| Prato | Scuola Comunale |
| PS | Biblioteca Cattedrale, Pistoia |
| PESc | Conservatorio di Musica Gioacchino Rossini, Pesaro |
| PLcon | Biblioteca Conservatorio Vincenzo Bellini, Palermo |
| Rasc | Archivio Storico Capitolino e Biblioteca Romana, Roma |
| REm | Biblioteca Municipale, Reggio Emilia |
| Ria | Istituto Nazionale di Archeologia e Storia delli Arte, Roma |
| Rf | Archivio dei Filippini, Roma |
| Rrostirolla | Biblioteca privata Giancarlo Rostirolla, Roma |
| Rvat | Biblioteca Apostolica Vaticana, Roma |
| RVE | Biblioteca Civica Girolamo Tartarotti, Rovereto |
| Spello | S. Lorenza Biblioteca, Spello |
| SI | Biblioteca Comunale, Siracusa |
| Tco | Biblioteca Conservatorio Statale eli Musica Giuseppe Verdi, Turin |
| Tf | Biblioteca Accademia Filarmonica, Turin |
| Tr | Biblioteca Reale, Turin |
| TE | Istituto Musicale G. Briccialdi, Terni |
| UDricardi | Biblioteca privata Federico Ricardi di Netro, Udine |
| URBcap | Biblioteca Capitolare (Duomo), Urbania |
| Vc | Biblioteca Conservatorio di Musica Benedetto Marcello, Venice |
| Vertova | Racoolta privata Belotti, Vertova |
| VEcap | Biblioteca Capitolare (Cattedrale), Verona |
| VD | Biblioteca Civica, Viadana |
| VIGsa | Biblioteca Duomo S. Ambrogio, Vigvano |
| Vlevi | Venezia, Biblioteca della Fondazione, "Ugo Levi" |
| Vmarcello | Biblioteca privata Andrighetti Marcello, Venice |
| Vnm | Biblioteca Nazionale Marciana, Venezia |
| Vsmc | Biblioteca S. Maria della Consolazione detta Della Fava, Venice |

## PL: POLAND

| | |
|---|---|
| PL: | Krakow: University Libraty |

# Acknowledgments

The reader is indebted for the second edition of this book
to Mr. Craig Dabelstein of Brisbane, Australia. Without his
contribution to design and all things involved as an editor this
book would never again have been available.

David Whitwell
Austin, 2012

# PART I
# The Renaissance

# The Renaissance

## Anonymous, 15th century

'*Mon cuor*'
MS   I:FZc (col. 117, 65v-66v), almost certainly for winds
     Includes an instrumental *Iaime* and a *Kyrie*

## Holborne, Antony (d. 1602)

*Pauans, Galliards, Almains, and other short Aeirs both graue, and light,*
   *in fiue parts, for Viols, Violins, or other Musicall Winde Instruments.*
EP   GB:Lbm (K.2.a.8.)

## Merulo, Claudio (1533–1604)

*Canzoni da suonare* a 4;
MS   I:VEcap (Cod.MCXXVIII)
     Contains:
     La Jussona a 4;
     La Rossa a 4;
     3 senza titolo.

# PART 2

# The Baroque

# Germany

**Anonymous**

*Sinfonia* in D
MS  302-1
    BRD:KA (Mus.Hs.1095)
    US:DW

*Concerto*
MS  302-
    BRD:HRD Fü (3720 a, 'No. 63')

*Concerto*
MS  302-1
    BRD:HRD Fü (3720 a, 'No. 135')

*Sonata*
MS  102-, with viol. di gamba
    BRD:HRD Fü (3720 a, 'No. 73')

*Sonata*
MS  2-
    BRD:HRD Fü (3720 a, 'No. 17')

*Solo Sonata*
MS  oboe and bc
    BRD:HRD Fü (3720 a, 'No. 21')

*Solo Sonata*
MS  flute and bc
    BRD:HRD Fü (3720 a, 'No. 33')

**Bach, J. S. (1685–1750)**

*Sonata*
MS  flute and basso
    BRD:HRD Fü (3720 a, 'No. 32')

**Bausteder, ?**

*Sonata*
MS  201-
    BRD:HRD Fü (3720 a, 'No. 35')

## Bigaglia, Diogenio (1676–1745)

*Concerto*
MS  401-
    BRD:HRD Fü (3720 a, 'No. 27')

## Califano, ?

*Sonata*
MS  201-
    BRD:HRD Fü (3720 a, 'No. 30')

*Sonata*
MS  202-
    BRD:HRD Fü (3720 a, 'No.8')

*Sonata*
MS  202-
    BRD:HRD Fü (3720 a, 'No.9')

*Sonata*
MS  202-
    BRD:HRD Fü (3720 a, 'No. 10')

*Sonata*
MS  202-
    BRD:HRD Fü (3720 a, 'No. 11')

## Fasch, Johann (1688–1758)

*Sonata*
MS  202-
    BRD:HRD Fü (3720 a, 'No. 61')

*Sonata*
MS  202-
    BRD:HRD Fü (3720 a, 'No. 12')

*Sonata*
MS  1201-,
    BRD:HRD Fü (3720 a, 'No. 23')

*Sonata*
MS  201-
    BRD:HRD Fü (3720 a, 'No. 24')

*Sonata*
MS 2-
    BRD:HRD Fü (3720 a, 'No. 12')

## Förster, Christoph (1693–1745)

*Concerto*
MS 501-
    BRD:HRD Fü (3720 a, 'No. 41 ')

*Concerto*
MS 302-
    BRD:HRD Fü (3720 a, 'No. 44')

## Graupner, Christoph (1683–1760)

*Ouverture* in F
MS 3 chalumeaux
    BRD:KA (Mus.Hs.183) [autograph]
    Seven movements: Ouverture, Gavotte, Air, Air, La Speranza, Air, and Minuet

## Heinichen, Johann David (1683–1729)

[3] *Solo Sonatas*
MS oboe, basso
    BRD:HRD Fü (3720 a, 'No. 20. 22. & 23')

## Hendel, ?

*Sonata*
MS 102-
    BRD:HRD Fü (3720 a, 'No. 6')

*Solo Sonata*
MS flute and bc
    BRD:HRD Fü (3720 a, 'No.3')

*Solo Sonata*
MS flute and basso
    BRD:HRD Fü (3720 a, 'No. 4')

## Linicke, Johann (b. ca. 1680)

*Sonata*
MS 102-
    BRD:HRD Fü (3720 a, 'No. 16')

*Duetto*
MS  2-
  BRD:HRD Fü (3720 a, 'No. 18')

*Duetto*
MS  2-
  BRD:HRD Fü (3720 a, 'No. 19')

## Molter, Johann Melchior (1696–1765)

*Sinfonia Concertante* in D
MS  201-12
  BRD:KA (Mus.Hs.317)

*Concerto* in D
MS  201-12
  BRD:KA (Mus.Hs.338)

[3] *Concerti*
MS  2001-2
  BRD:KA (Mus.Hs.373–375)

*Quartet*
MS  -22
  BRD:KA (Mus.Hs.444)

*Quartet*
MS  4 winds and bass
  BRD:KA (Mus.Hs.445)

[4] *Märsche*
MS  212-02
  BRD:KA (Mus.Hs.448)

[4] *Märsche*
MS  202-02
  BRD:KA (Mus.Hs.449)

*Sonata*
MS  21-02
  BRD:KA (Mus.Hs.508)

*Sonata*
MS  202-2
  BRD:KA (Mus.Hs.509)

*Symphonia* (4 mvts)
MS  201-1
    BRD:KA (Mus.Hs.673)

*Symphonia* (3 movements, incomplete)
MS  201-02
    BRD:KA (Mus.Hs.675)

[2] *Symphoniae* in D
MS  201-1
    BRD:KA (Mus.Hs.546–547)

[2] *Symphoniae* in D
MS  2001-02
    BRD:KA (Mus.Hs.596–597)

*Symphoniae* (4 movements)
MS  -04
    BRD:KA (Mus.Hs.667)

## Praetorius, Michael (1571–1621)

*Polyhymnia Caduceatrix & Panegyrica* ... Solennische ... Concert...mit allerhandt Musica-
lischen Instrumenten vnd Menschen Stimmen, auch Trommetten vnd Heer-Paucken
Musiciret ...
EP  (Wolffenbüttel, 1619)
    GB:Lbm (G.131.)

## Quantz, Johann (1697–1773)

*Sonata*
MS  201-
    BRD:HRD Fü (3720 a, 'No. 28')

*Sonata*
MS  2001-
    BRD:HRD Fü (3720 a, 'No. 29')

*Sonata*
MS  2-
    BRD:HRD Fü (3720 a, 'No. 13')

## Stühl, ?

*Sonata*
MS  2-
    BRD:HRD Fü (3720 a, 'No. 14')

*Solo Sonata*
MS  1-
   BRD:HRD Fü (3720 a, 'No. 15')

## Telemann, Georg (1681–1767)

*Sonate*
MS  2001-
   BRD:HRD Fü (3720 a, 'No. 88')

*Sonata*
MS  1101-
   BRD:HRD Fü (3720 a, 'No. 1')

*Sonata*
MS  oboe and bc
   BRD:HRD Fü (3720 a, 'No. 6')

## Werner, Gregor (1695–1766)

*Sonata*
MS  202-
   BRD:HRD Fü (3720 a, 'No. 15')

# Great Britain

## Anonymous

*Mars, his Triumph*. Or, ... an exercise performed the XVIII of October, 1638, in the Merchant-Taylors Hall (With the music of three marches)
EP   (London, 1639)
    GB:Lbm (8828.ee.3.)

## Jordan, Thomas

*The Goldsmiths Jubile: or Londons Triumphs*: containing A Description of the several Pageants ... Performed October 29, 1674, for the Entertainment of ... Lord Mayor.
EP   (London, 1674)
    GB:Lbm (577.d.41.)

*London's Glory*, or, the Lord Mayor's Show: containing an Illustrious Description of the several Triumphant Pageants ... to be Sung or Play'd. Performed on October 29, 1680.
EP   (London, 1680)
    GB:Lbm (113.1.20.)

## Tutors

*The Compleat Tutor for the French Horn*. Containing the best and easiest Instructions for Leaners ... To which are added all the Hunting Notes and several choice Lessons for one and two French Horns.
EP   (London, 1746)
    GB:Lbm (d.47.f.[5.])

*The Compleat Tutor for the German Flute*, containing ... instructions ... Translated from the French. To which is added a choice collection of ... Italian, English & Scotch tunes.
EP   (London, 1745)
    GB:Lbm (d.150.b.)

*The Compleat Tutor to the Hautboy*; or the Art of playing on that instrument improved and made easy ... by very plain rules and directions for learners. Also a choice collection of trumpett-tunes, ayres, marches & minuetts. Composed by the best masters.
EP   (London, 1715)
    GB:Lbm (K.4.a.19.)

# Italy

**Anonymous**

*Credo* in G (1742)
MS  4 voices, flutes, oboes, horns, viole (?), organ
    I:Vsmc

**Albinoni, Tommaso (1671–1750)**

*Concerto*
MS  302-, 'alto'
    BRD:HRD Fü (3720 a, 'No. 66')

*Sonata*
MS  oboe and basso
    BRD:HRD Fü (3720 a, 'No. 27')

**Feo, Francesco (1691–1761)**

*Dixit*
MS  SSTB, 200-02
    I:Nf

**Lotti, Antonio (1667–1740)**

*Echo*
MS  202-
    BRD:HRD Fü (3720 a, 'No. 6')

*Sonata*
MS  202-
    BRD:HRD Fü (3720 a, 'No.7')

**Porpora, Nicola (1686–1776, Haydn's teacher)**

*Ouverture Roiale* (1763)
MS  202-22, timpani
    I:Nc (19.5.25) [autograph score]; US:DW (1399)

**Sammartini, Giovanni Battisti (1698–1775)**

*Concertino* in G (2 movements)
MS   202-02
   BRD:KA (Mus.Hs.792)

*Concertino* in C (1 movement)
MS   2201-22
   BRD:KA (Mus.Hs.782)
   BRD:KA (Mus.Hs.794) [for 2 vln, bass]
   BRD:KA (Mus.Hs.783) [for 2201-22]

*Concertino* in G (1 movement)
MS   2201-22
   BRD:KA (Mus.Hs.788)

**Vivaldi, Antonio (1675–1741)**

*Concerto*, Nr. 47
MS   concertino: 2 ob, 2 hn, 'viol.'
   I:Vc (Torrefranca-Cart.Mss.12)

*Concerto*, Nr. 48
MS   concertino: 2 ob, 2 hn, 'viol.'
   I:Vc (Torrefranca-Cart.Mss.11)

*Sonata*
MS   1102-
   BRD:HRD Fü (3720 a, 'No. 14')

PART 3

# The Classical Period

# Austria

**Bruzzeh [Brusek], Joseph**

*Salve regina*
MS  SAT, 222-02
    I:MOe (Mus.D.38)

**Haydn, Franz Josef (1732–1809)**

*Andante*
MS  2 horns
    I:Tf (11.II.1-12,5)

3 *Duetti*
MS  2 oboes
    I:Mc (A/33/16/2)

6 *Duetti*
MS  2 oboes
    I:Mc (A/33/16/1)

**Kreith, Karl (1746–1809)**

*Divertimento*
MS  -02, organ
    I:OS (Mss.Mus.B.1184) [this is a reduction from the original *Quintet* for 21-02, by
    Giuseppe Greggiati (1793–1866)]

*Partita* in C
MS  222-02
    I:Gl (ss.B.1.10.H.8)

**Mozart, Wolfgang Amadeus (1756–1791)**

*Tito*
MS  eight-part Harmoniemusik
    I:BGc (Mayr.E.1.4); I:MOe (Mus.D.262) [Krechtler]

*Sei Marce per amonia*
MS
    I:Ria (Ms.16)

*Partita* in C Minor, K.384a
MS  222-02
    I:BGc (Faldone 243.18) [Anesa]
EP  (Offenbach: André, 1811, ,d' apres le manuscrit de l'auteur')
    GB:Lbm (h.405.q.[2.])

*Partita* in E♭, K.375
EP  (Offenbach, André, 1792)
    GB:Lbm (h.405.y.)
EP  (Vienna: Artaria, 1799, for string quintet)
    GB:Lbm (H.3690.m.)

*Gran Partita* in B♭, K.370a
EP  (Offenbach, André, 1801, arr. for orchestra by F. Gleissner)
    GB:Lbm (Hirsch M.1109)
EP  (Bonn: Simrock, 1830, arr. for four-hand piano)
    GB:Lbm (f.67.q.[4.])

*Marcia*
MS
    I:Ria (Ms.411)

*Jupiter Symphony*
EP  19th century arr. for large band (Milano, 1903)
    I:Mc (A.45.27.9) [Movements I & II]
    I:Mc (A.45.27.10) [Movements III & IV]

## Pleyel, Ignaz (1757–1831)

*Due Quintetti*
MS  21-02
    I:UDricardi (Ms.147) [parts]

## Weigl, Joseph (1766–1846)

*Nachtigall und Raabe*
MS  Harmoniemusik (arr. Starbe)
    I:BGc (Mayr.E.2.8)

## Winter, Peter (1754–1825)

*Das Labyrinth*
MS  Harmoniemusik
    I:BGc (Mayr.E.1.37)

*Serenate*
MS   Harmoniemusik
    I:Fc (D.V.558)

## Wranitzky, Paul (1756–1808)

*Nosen armonica*
MS   six-part Harmoniemusik
    I:CRg (Pia Instit.Musicale) [score]

## Wranitzky, Wenzel

*Trios*
MS   21-
    I:UDricardi (mss 99) [also more under Mss.100 and Mss.101]

# France

**Anonymous**

*Ordonance Militaire de l'École des Trompettes*
EP   (Paris, 1794)
     GB:Lbm (G.554.a.[5.])

**Blasius, Matthieu (1758–1829)**

*Messe en harmonie* in C
MS  SAB, 1031-121, bass drun
     I:Mc (Noseda) [parts, probably autograph]

**Della Maria, Pierre-Antoine (1769–1800)**

*Der Gefangene* (*Le Prisonnier*)
MS  222-02 (arr.)
     I:Fc (530)

**Eler, Andreas (1764–1821)**

3 *Quartetti*
MS  1011-01
     I:Ria (Ms.629)

**Lefèvre, Jean Xavier (1763–1829)**

*Mere commune des hunains* (for chorus and band)
EP   (Paris, 1796)
     GB:Lbm (E.1717.b.[32.])

**Méhul, Étienne (1763–1817)**

*Le Chant des Victoires* (for chorus and band)
EP   (Paris, 1794)
     GB:Lbm (E.1717.b.[4.])
     GB:Lbm (645.a.41.[22.])

*Le Chant du Retour* (for chorus and band)
EP   (Paris, 1797)
     GB:Lbm (E.1717.b.[41.])

*Chant Funèbre a la memoire ... Ferraud* (for chorus and band)
EP   (Paris, 1795)
     GB:Lbm (823.1.17.[14.])
     GB:Lbm (Hirsch IV.847)

*Overture*
EP   (London, 1877)
     GB:Lbm (f.411.b.[18.])

*L'Hyme des Vingt Deux* (for chorus and band)
EP   (Paris, 1795)
     GB:Lbm (E.1717.b.[22.])

*Die Beiden Fuchse*
MS   nine-part Harmoniemusik
     I:BGc (Mayr.E.1.6)

*Joseph und seine Bruder*
MS   Harmoniemusik
     I:BGc (Mayr.E.2.20)

# Germany

**Anonymous**

*Divertimento* in D
MS  -04
    BRD:KA (Mus.Hs.1089)

*Marsch* in D
MS  201-02, timp
    BRD:KA (Mus.Hs.1072)

*Partitta* in D (4 movements)
MS  2001-02
    BRD:KA (Mus.Hs.1087)

*Partitta* in G (6 movements)
MS  201-02
    BRD:KA (Mus.Hs.1085)

*Partitta* in F (8 mvts)
MS  solo clarinet, 201-02
    BRD:KA (Mus.Hs.1084)

*Partitta* (7 movements)
MS  solo clarinet, 201-02
    BRD:KA (Mus.Hs.1082)

*Partitta* in B♭ (8 movements)
MS  201-02
    BRD:KA (Mus.Hs.1083)

*Partitta* in C (7 movements)
MS  201-02
    BRD:KA (Mus.Hs.1081)

*Partitta* in D (6 movements)
MS  201-02
    BRD:KA (Mus.Hs.1080)

*Sonata* (3 mts)
MS  -04
    BRD:KA (Mus.Hs.1088)

## Danzi, Franz (1763–1826)

*Sextett* in E♭
MP  (Hanburg: Sikorski, 1965)
  BRD:KA (M.1156)

*Herr Gott, Dich loben wir*, in E♭
MS  SATB, 2-22, 2 celli, bass, organ
  BRD:Sl (H.B.XVII, Nr. 127.a.b.)

## Feldnayr, Georg (1756–1818)

*Parthia* in D
MS  2222-02
  BRD:HR (III.4.1/2.20.589)

*Parthia* in F
MS  2222-03, bass
  BRD:HR (III.4.1/2.20.595)

*Parthia* in F
MS  201-02
  BRD:HR (III.4.1/2.20.474)

*Serenata* in D
MS  1212-13, bass
  BRD:HR (III.4.1/2.20.596)

## Hasse, Johann Adolf (1699–1783)

*Crucifixus*
MS  T, Contratenor, 21-, be
  I:Vc (Ospedaletto VII, 121)

*Marcia*
MS  201-02
  I:Mc (Noseda) [listed in one catalog, but I could not find this work in the Noseda collection.]

## Hiebesch, Johann (1766–1820)

*Parthia* in F
MS  1212-03, bass
  BRD:HR (III.4.1/2.20.608)

## Hoffneister, Franz Anton (1754–1812)

*Sestetto*
MS  22-02
   I:Gl (Sc.128)

## Reicha, Joseph (1746–1795)

*Parthia* in D
MS  2222-02, bass
   BRD:HR (III.4.1/2.40.94)

*Parthia* in D
MS  2222-02, bass
   BRD:HR (III.4.1/2.20.477)

## Schneider, ?

*Partita* in C
MS  1-02, 2 Eng. hn
   BRD:HR (III.4.1/2.20.723)

## Scholl, Nikolaus

*Musikalischer Sammler für die Harmonie eigerichtet*
MS  10 winds
   I:MOe (Mus.F.1409-10)

## Schön, ?

*Quartet*
MS  12-01
   I:Mc (Da Camera Ms. 26.2)

## Vanderhagen, Amand (1753–1822)

*Pezzi d'Armonia*
MS  22-02
   I:G1 (SS.B.1.13)
   Apparently consists of arrangements of the operas, *L'Italianain Londra*, *Giannina e Bernardone*, and *Schiavi d'amore*.

**Weideman, Carl Friedrich (d. 1782)**

*The Old Buffs March*
EP   (Dublin, 1760)
   GB:Lbm (h.141.h. [5.])

**Witt, Friedrich (1771–1837)**

*Pieces d'Harmonie*
MS   32-121, serpent
   I:Ria (mss.271) [score]

# Great Britain

## Anonymous

*Eleven Anthems* on General and Particular Occasions, interspersed with Symphonies and
    Thorough Basses, for Two Hautboys and a Bassoon
EP   (London, 1790)
    GB:Lbm (G.521.a.)

*The Arch Duke Charles of Austria March*
EP   (London, 1797)
    GB:Lbm (g.133.[72.])

*Bellisle March and the Retreat*, as performed before his Majesty ... 27, June, 1763.
EP   (London, 1763)
    GB:Lbm (G.316.d.[166.])
    GB:Lbm (H.1994.a.[215.])

*Captain Reed's or the Third Regiment of Guards March*
EP   (London, 1770)
    GB:Lbm (H.1994.a.[176.])

*Coldstream, or Second Regiment of Guards March*
EP   (London, 1770)
    GB:Lbm (H.1994.a.[180.])

*A Second Collection of XXIV Favourite Marches* in 7 Parts
EP   (London, 1771)
    GB:Lbm (a.226.)

*The Duke of Glosters March*
EP   (London, 1765)
    GB:Lbm (H.1994.a.[214.])

*The Egyptian March*
EP   (London, 1800)
    GB:Lbm (h.1568.b.[13.])

*XXIV favourite Marches* in five parts (for 2 violins, flutes, or oboes, with two horns
    and bassoon)
EP   (London, 1765) [missing the horn and bassoon parts]
    GB:Lbm

*General Suwarrow's March & Quick Step* ... to which is added five Russian Dances
EP   (Edinburgh, 1798)
    GB:Lbm (h.1568.b.[11.])

*Three Grand Marches, and three Quick Steps*, for a full Military Band by an Eminent Master
EP   (London, 1800)
    GB:Lbm (R.M.15.g.11.)

*The Grand Neapolitan March*
EP   (London, 1800)
    GB:Lbm (h.1568.b.[12.])

*Princess Charlotte of Wale's Troop*
EP   (London, 1800)
    GB:Lbm (g.1780.nn.[17.])

*Lord Lewisham's March* as performed by the Staffordshire Militia
EP   (London, 1780)
    GB:Lbm (g.271.t.[13.])

*March of the Thirty-fifth Regiment*
EP   (London, 1780)
    GB:Lbm (I.600.d.[110.])

*The Prince of Brunswick' s March*
EP   (London)
    GB:Lbm (H.1601.a.[114.])

*Royal Westminster Regiment of Militia March*
EP   (London, 1790)
    GB:Lbm (g.352.ii.[19.])

[4] *Marches for the Volunteer Corps of the County of Down*
EP   (Dublin, 1780)
    GB:Lbm (H.1601.a.[115.])

*Four Quick Marches*
EP   (London, 1800)
    GB:Lbm (g.137.[29.])

## Hill, Frederick

*A Favourite Quick Step*, for Clarinets, French Horns and Bassoons
EP   (London, 1795)
    GB:Lbm (g.133.[26.])

## Hoeberechts, John Lewis (1760–1820)

*A Grand Military Piece* (for 4 cl., 2 hns., 2 bsns., and serpent)
EP   (London, 1799)
   GB:Lbm (h.3213.k.[7.])

## Hummell, Charles

*Les Delassements Militaires* ('for a full military band')
EP   (London, 1800)
   GB:Lbm (g.137.[30.]) [here for piano and harp]

## Hyde, Janes ('Trumpet Major')

*A New and Compleat Preceptor for the Trumpet & Bugle Horn* with ... the Cavalry Duty ... to
   which is added a Selection of Airs, Marches & Quick Steps for Three Trumpets ...
EP   (London, 1799)
   GB:Lbm (b.133.[1])

## Instructions

*Complete Instructions for the Bassoon*, Containing the most useful Directions & Examples ... to
   Obtain a Proficiency: To which is Annexed ... A Selection of the most Admired Songs,
   Airs, Duetts, etc.
EP   (London, 1790)
   GB:Lbm (b.160.g.[2.])

*Compleat Instructions for the Bassoon or Fagotto* ... To which are added a curious collection of
   tunes & duets for one & two bassoons
EP   (London, 1780)
   GB:Lbm (c.250.n.)

*Compleat Instructions for the Bassoon or Fagotto*
EP   (London, 1800)
   GB:Lbm (b.160.s.)

*Compleat Instructions for the Clarinet*, containing an accurate Drawing ... with the modern graces & improvements. To which is added a collection of modern popular airs,
   marches, duets, etc., and a concise dictionary of musical terms
EP   (London, 1785)
   GB:Lbm (b.160.1.)

*Compleat Instructions for the Common Flute* ... To which is added a favorite collection of
   Minuets, Marches, Song Tunes, etc., Properly disposed for that instrument
EP   (London, 1780)
   GB:Lbm (b.170.c.)

*Compleat Instructions for the Fife* … to which is added a favourite collection of the most celebrated marches, airs, duets, etc., Perform'd in the Guards, Militia and other regiments
EP  (London, 1795)
    GB:Lbm (c.250.z.[1.])

*Compleat Instructions for the German Flute* … To which is added, a favourite collection of
minuets, marches, song tunes, & duets
EP  (London, 1767)
    GB:Lbm (b.170.i.)

*Compleat Instructions for the German Flute* … To which is added, a collection of minuets,
marches, song tunes, etc.
EP  (London, 1768)
    GB:Lbm (b.170.g.)

*Compleat Instructions for the German Flute* … carefully corrected by the most eminent masters,
to which is added, a favourite Collection of Minuets, Marches, Song Tunes, Duetts, etc.
EP  (London, 1770)
    GB:Lbm (a.50.)

*Entire new and compleat Instructions for the Fife* … with a collection of … marches , airs, etc.,
perform'd in the Guards and other regiments
EP  (London, 1785)
    GB:Lbm (b.160.o.)

*Modem Instructions for the German Flute*
EP  (London, 1800)
    GB:Lbm (a.19.g.[1.])

*New and Compleat Instructions for the Clarionet*, Containing the Easiest & most Improved
Rules for Learners to Play, to which is added a Selection of Songs, Airs, Minuets,
Marches, Duetts, etc.
EP  (London, 1798)
    GB:Lbm (b.160.g.[1.])

*New and complete Instructions for the Common Flute* … to which is added a favorite collection
of songs, airs, minuets, marches, duets, etc.
EP  (London, 1790)
    GB:Lbm (b.160.p.)

*New and complete Instructions for the Oboe or Hoboy* … To which is added a select collection of
airs, marches, minuets, duets, etc., also the favorite rondeau performed at Vauxhall by
Mr. Fischer
EP  (London, 1770)
    GB:Lbm (b.160.r.)

*New and Complete Instructions for the Oboe or Hoboy* … To which is added A selection collection of Airs, Marches, Minuets, Duets, etc., also the favorite Rondeaus performed at Vauxhall by Mr. Fischer
EP  (London, 1780)
    GB:Lbm (b.160.h.)

*New and Complete Instructions for the Hautboy* … To which is added a favorite collection of Airs, Marches, Minuets, Duets, etc., Also the favorite Rondo performed at Vauxhall by Mr. Fischer
EP  (London, 1790)
    GB:Lbm (b.160.c.[3.])

*New Instructions for the French Horn*, containing the most modern and best methods for leamers to blow, to which are added, all the hunting notes, and a collection of tunes, marches, minuets, etc., adapted by an eminent performer
EP  (London, 1780)
    GB:Lbm (b.160.t.)

*New Instructions for the German Flute* … To which is added a favorite Collection of Minuets, Marches, Song Tunes, Duets, etc. Also the method of double Tongueing and a description of a new invented German-Flute play'd on by Florio and Tacet
EP  (London, 1775)
    GB:Lbm (b.170.b.[2.])

*New Instructions for the German Flute* … To which is added a favorite Collection of Minuets, Marches, Song Tunes, Duets, etc.
EP  (London, 1780)
    GB:Lbm (b.400.d.[2.])

*New Instructions for the German-Flute* … to which is added a favorite Collection of Minuets, Marches, Song Tunes, Duets, etc. Also the method of double Tongueing and a description of a new invented German Flute such as play'd on by Florio and Tacet
EP  (London, 1790)
    GB:Lbm (a.243.)

## Jouve, Joseph

*The Austrian Retreat*
EP  (London, 1800)
    GB:Lbm (h.1480.x.[15.])

*Twelve Military Divertimentos* for the Forte Piano or Harp, consisting of Marchs, Airs, Waltz's and Quick Steps. Principaly composed and adapted for … the Prince of Wales.
EP  (London, 1800)
    GB:Lbm (R.M.17.f.14.[8.])

## Leach, Thomas

*The Harfield Royal Review*
EP   (London, 1801)
   GB:Lbm (h.61.h.[10.])

## Pick, Henry

*Harmonie* ... selected from the Works of celebrated Composers and arranged for four Clari-
   nets, two Flutes, two French horns, two Bassoons, Serpent or Trombono, Bugle Horn,
   Trumpet and Bass Drum
EP   (London, 1797)
   GB:Lbm (R.M.17.f.10.[1.])

*A set of Favorite Military Divertisements*, Op. 4
EP   (London, 1800)
   GB:Lbm (h.141.o.) [missing all but the tambourin part]

## Spencer, John

*The Favorite Troop* performed by the Band of the Oxford Shire Militia
EP   (London, 1795)
   GB:Lbm (h.1568.b.[21.])

## Worgan, Janes, Jr. (1715–1753)

*A March composed for the Loyal Essex Regiment of Fencible Infantry*
EP   (London, 1801)
   GB:Lbm (g.133.[67.])

# Italy

**Anonymous**

*Twenty-four Italian Pieces*, being Marches, Minuets, Airs, etc., in seven parts viz two horns,
  two G flutes, two clarinets, oboes or violins, a bassoon or violoncello, etc.
EP  (London: Longman Lukey & Co., ca. 1770)
    GB:Lbm (b.78.a.) [here the flute parts only]

*Gloria*
MS  TTB, 201-02, organ
    I:Vc (Ospedaletto II, 25)

*Gloria in excelsis* (Mottetto) in C
MS  voices, bassoon, trombones, bass
    I:Fa

*Gratias*
MS  T solo, 101-02, organ
    I:Vc (Ospedaletto II, 27)

*Marcia* (on a theme from Mozart's *Marriage of Figaro*)
MS  222-12
    I:Tf (0.II.14-3)

*Sinfonia* in C
MS  2 horns and basso
    I:OS (Ms.Mus.B.4682)

*Sonata* in C
MS  2 horns, contrabasso, organ
    I:OS (Ms.Mus.B.573)

Suite di 7 pezzi in Eb
MS  122-02
    I:BGc (Faldone 252.20) [Anesa]

**Aber, Giovanni**

6 *Sonate*
MS  2002-02
    I:Mc (Noseda A-1-12)

## Adler, ?

*6 Quintetti*
MS 21-02
    I:UDricardi (Mus.145)

## Altafulla, Ubaldo (fl. 1800–1810)

*Messa*
MS 3 voices e strumenti a fiato
    I:Bsf

## Arici, Marco (1778–1827)

*Cum Sancto*
MS SATB, 1020-121, org.
    I:BGi (Fondo Cappella Basilica S. Maria Maggiore, Faldone 24, n. 1035) [Anesa]

*Concertino* per Oboe in D
MS oboe, 2021-02
    I:Colombaro-Bibl. priv. Barcella (48)

## Bertoni, Ferdinando G. (1725–1813)

*Beatus vir*
MS TTB, 200-02, org
    I:Vs

*Credo*
MS TTB, 5 winds
    I:Chioggia:Filippini

*Kyrie*
MS TTB, 9 winds, timp
    I:Chioggia:Filippini

*Kyrie*
MS TTB, 17 winds
    I:Chioggia:Filippini

*Pastorale e Gloria*
MS SATB, 2201-02, org, viola (talia?)
    I:Bc (DD.150)

## Bihler, Franz (1760–1824)

*Gold lacht der Lag* (Cantata, 1797)
MS  SSTB, 2221-12
    I:BZtoggenburg (A/V, 56)

*Heil und dank den Sieger* (Cantata, in C)
MS  SATB, 2221-12
    I:BZtoggenburg (A/V, 52)

*Pange lingua*
MS  SATB, 2222-02
    I:BZtoggenburg (A/V, 4)

*Pange lingua*
MS  SATB, 1022-221, piccolo, timp.
    I:BZtoggenburg (A/V, 2)

*Tantum Ergo*
MS  SATB, Solo Eng. hn, 2022-22, org., timp.
    I:BZtoggenburg (A/V, 38)

*Tantum Ergo* (1796)
MS  SATB, 2202-02, st. bass
    I:BZtoggenburg (A/V, 32)

## Bisoni, Antonio (fl. ca. 1784)

*Iste confessor*
MS  3 voices, 2101-02, org.
    I:FZac (Busta 2, 21)

## Boccherini, Luigi (1743–1805)

6 *Fughe per due Fagotti*
MS  2 bsns
    I:Vc (2315)

## Bonacci, Francesco

*Mottetti*
MS  voices and winds
    I:Rf (H.iv.6a)

### Bonari, Guierriero (fl. ca. 1820)

*Messa* in C
MS  STB, 1020-02, bc
    I:BGc (Mayr.64.1)

### Borghi, Giovanni (1713–1796)

*Litanie* della B. V. in B♭ (1794)
MS  TTB, 122-02
    I:REm (mus.sacra LXXX-I)

*Litanie* in B♭
MS  Voices and winds
    I:Vsmc

### Brunetti, Giovanni Gualberto (1715–1808)

*Messa*
MS  4 voices, winds
    I:Gl (P.B.4.1.D.8.2)

*Notte serena e placida*
MS  3 voices, flutes, horns, basso
    I:Fc (D.IV.52)

### Cocchi, Gioachino (1715–1804)

*Duet*, 'Deb resplendi, o chiaro nume'
MS  SS, flutes, trombones
    I:Fc (D.IV.48)

### Domenichini, Antonio (fl. ca. 1770)

2 *Notturni*, in D, G
MS  2000-02, viola, bass
    I:Gl (SS.B.1.4)

*Sonata notturna* in D
MS  201-02
    I:PS (Rospigliosi)

### Furlanetto, Bonaventura (1730–1817)

*Credo*
MS  SSB, 102-12, org.
    I:Vc (Ospadeletto, V, 88)

*Kyrie*
MS  SSB, 102,12, org.
  I:Vc (Ospadeletto, V, 99)

*Kyrie e Gloria* in F
MS  TB, winds, org.
  I:Chioggia-Filippini

*Pange lingua* in G (1799)
MS  SSB, 202-02
  I:Nc (mus.relig.627)

*Pange lingua*
MS  4 voices, winds
  I:Vnm (Cod.It.IV-730)

(3) *Tantum ergo* in C, D, A minor
MS  TTB, winds, org.
  I:Chiogga-Filippini

*Tantum ergo*
MS  3 voices, 100-02, organ
  I:Vc (Ospedaletto, VI, 115)

*Tantum ergo* in C (1790)
MS  3 voices, 100-02, org.
  I:Vsmc

*Tantum ergo* in C
MS  TTT, winds, org.
  I:Chioggia-Filippini

## Gandini, Antonio

*Erminia*
MS  2222-02, contrabsn
  I:MOe (Mus.F.1727)
  Based on *Die beiden Eraniten*, by Gyrowetz.

## Gherardi, Gherardo

*Salve regina* in E♭ (1799)
MS  SSATB, 222-02
  I:PAc

## Lenzi, Carlo (1735–1805)

*Ave maris stella*, in D, per processione (1780)
MS  SATB, 201-02
 I:BGi (Fondo Cappella Basilica S. Maria Maggiore, Faldone 6, n. 56.73) [Anesa]

*Ave maris stella*, in C, per processione (1795)
MS  SATB, 201-02, timp, cont.
 I:BGi (Fondo Cappella Basilica S. Maria Maggiore, Faldone 6, n. 58.74) [Anesa]

*Ave maris stella*, in F, per processione (1791)
MS  SATB, 201-, org.
 I:BGi (Fondo Cappella Basilica S. Maria Maggiore, Faldone 6, n. 60) [Anesa]

*Laudate pueri* in F
MS  SAB, 201-02
 I:BGi (Fondo Cappella Basilica S. Maria Maggiore, Faldone 23, n. 256) [Anesa]

*Pange lingua* in C (1794)
MS  SATB, 222-02
 I:BGi (Fondo Cappella Basilica S. Maria Maggiore, Faldone 28, n. 298.75) [Anesa]

*Sanctorum meritis*, concertato per la processione de S. Fermo in D
MS  SATB, 202-02
 I:BGi (Fondo Cappella Basilica S. Maria Maggiore, Faldone 29, n. 318.76) [Anesa]

## Moneta, Giuseppe (1754–1806)

*Musica per Banda e Corio … Allegorica nella feste* (5 July, 1791)
MS  band and chorus
 I:Fc (A.246)

## Nappi, Emanuele (1767–1836)

*La Marchia di Gesu Christo al Calvario*
MS  clarinets, horns, trumpet, basso
 I:AN (Ms.Mus.54)

## Piazza, Felici

(12) *Quintetti*
MS  21-02
 I:Mc (Noseda 0.7.11)

## Sarti, Giuseppi (1729–1802)

*Marcia* (in 4 tempi) in C
MS  2122-12
    I:FZc (Ms.32.2)

## Storaro, ?

*Marcia* in me bem.
MS  organ and 11 winds
    I:Vsmc

## Tassoni, Clemente

*Marcia funebre dei dilettanti di Viadana*
MS  band (?)
    I:VD (I.6) [score] (perhaps I:UD)

## Vignali, Gabriele, fl. c. 1770

*Piaghe ador ate*
MS  TTB con strumenti a fiato
    I:Bc

# Poland

**Czeyka, Valentin (b. 1769)**

*Ländler*
MS   32-22
    I:Mc (Noseda E. 67-2)

PART 4

# The Nineteenth Century

# Austria [including Hungarian and Bohemian composers]

**Diabelli, Anton (1781–1858)**

*Triumph. Einzug der Verbundeten Michte in Paris*
MS  Harmoniemusik
    I:BGc (Mayr.E.27)

**Fahrbach, Philip, Jr. (1843–1894)**

*Walzer per Banda*
MS  band
    I:OS (Mss.Mus.B.4850)

*Farfadet*, Polka
EP  (London, 1889)
    GB:Lbn (h.1544.)

*Mazurka*, 'Roses blanches'
EP  (London, 1896)
    GB:Lbm (h.1549)

**Gung' l, Joseph (1810–1889)**

*Symphonic Tone Poem*, Op. 103
EP  (London, 1879)
    GB:Lbm (h.1549.)

**Hummel, Johann Nepomuk (1778–1837)**

*Die Eselshaut oder Die Blau Insel*
MS  Harmoniemusik
    I:BGc (Mayr.E.2.5)

*Helene et Paris*
MS  Harmoniemusik
    I:BGc (Mayr.E.2.2)

*Marsch für das Löbl:* Bürgl: Artillerie Corps in Wien
EP  (Vienna [?], 1798)
    GB:Lbm [e.5.h.(2.)]

## Joachim, Johann (an Austrian bandsman stationed in Mantua)

*Deutsche* (1823)
MS  seven-part Harmoniemusik
    I:OS (Mss.Musiche.B.4797)

*7 Deutsche stücke* (1826)
MS  2020-12, percussion
    I:OS (Mss.Mus.B.1180)

*Marcia*
MS  winds
    I:OS (Mss.Mus.B.509)

Nr. 2 *Marcie*
MS  Bassoon, trombones, tuba
    I:OS (Mss.Mus.B.1179) [bsn, trombones, tuba; additional parts under Mss.
    Mus.B.2227, 3644, and 4818]

## Kéler, Béla (1820–1882)

The following works were published, 1871–1907, in London.

*Alpers Lust*, Landler
    GB:Lbm (h.1549.)

*Am schönen Rhein gedenk ich dein*, Valse
    GB:Lbm (h.1549.)

*Deutsches Gemüthsleben* Valse
EP  (London, 1874)
    GB:Lbm (h.1549.])

*Französische Lustspiel-Overture*, Op. 111
    GB:Lbm (h.1549.)

*Grand Galop infernal*, Op. 60
    GB:Lbm (h.1549.)

*L'Hirondelle Polka*
    GB:Lbm (h.1549.)

*Hurra, Hurra, Hurra, Grand Storm Galop*, Op. 12
    GB:Lbm (h.1549.)

*Jubiläumsfeier,* Festival Overture
    GB:Lbm (h.1549.)

*Lustspiel-Overture*, Op. 73
   GB:Lbm (h.1549.)

*Ouverture comique*, Op. 74
   GB:Lbm (h.1549.)

*Ouverture romantique*, Op. 75
   GB:Lbm (h.1549.)

Galop, 'Rotten Row'
   GB:Lbm (h.1549)

*Ungarische Lustspiel-Overture*, Op. 108
   GB:Lbm (h.1549.)

*Vom Rhein zur Donau*, Valse
   GB:Lbm (h.1549.)

*Wiesbadner* quick march
   GB:Lbm (f.401.m.[9.])

## Komzak, Karl (1823–1893)

*Rabin Libejicer* (Polka)
EP   (London, 1880)
   GB:Lbm (h.1549)

## Kromner, Franz (1759–1831)

### On the Milano–Krommer scores

Franz Krommer began his residence in Vienna in 1795, where for three years his primary income seems to have been in private teaching. His first aristocratic employment appears to have been in the household of the Duke Ignaz Fuchs, from 1798 to 1810. It would seem most likely that his finest examples of *Harmoniemusik* were written between 1795 and 1810 for after 1810 his official court employments, Concertmeister for the court ballet, 1811–1815, and 'Chamber door guardian' to the Emperor Franz I, after 1815, involved devoting his time in entirely new directions and in the latter position much travel.

The earliest of the outstanding Viennese partitas by Krommer are the Op. 45 group of three, published in 1803 by the Bureau d'Arts et d'Industrie in Vienna. These were composed for the Archduke Joseph, Palatine of Hungary and a son to the Emperor Leopold II in Vienna as were some of the later partitas (Op. 67 and Op. 69). This is no surprise as it was the royal family in Vienna which was at the center of the new *Harmoniemusik* movement.

The great group of mature partitas, Op. 57, 67, 69, 71, 73, 76, 77, 78, 79 and 83, all appear to have been published in Vienna before 1810, in sets of parts without scores. Because of the great quality of these partitas it has followed that persons even up to the present day have had to invest the labor of creating scores from these early parts. It was actually a very long tradition, that once works were published the autograph scores were thrown away. It is for this reason that of the thousands of madrigals and canzoni of the late Italian sixteenth century there is hardly a single manuscript to be found. In a later example, once his copyist had created a presentation score of his great work for band, the *Siegessinfonie*, and Beethoven had proofed it, his autograph score was disposed of as no longer needed.

It was then of great interest to me that in 1989 while doing research in Milan I found a set of early scores for Op. 57, 67, 69, 77, 78, 79 and 83 in the very neat calligraphy that scholars refer to as 'presentation scores.' I did not have at hand a copy of Krommer's calligraphy when he was making clean copies for gifts, but my eye was immediately drawn to the very idiosyncratic style of writing the bass F Clef which I had found in other Krommer manuscripts.

I was excited to think that Harmoniemusik scores contemporary with Krommer had at last been found and I quickly spread the word to the other scholars and musicians interested in these partitas. The first other scholar to go to Milan to study these scores was Bastiaan Blomhert. He was able to determine that the handwriting was in the hand of a Viennese physician, Peter Lichtenthal, who had moved to Milan in 1810 where today he is represented by a large collection of his other scores. Blomhert further concluded that the scores were made from the published parts by Steiner in Vienna (which in turn were based on earlier Viennese publications) because grammatical errors found in the Milan scores are also (previously) found in the Steiner parts.

But, of course, it could have been the other way around. Those errors could have been first in the Lichtenthal scores, if they were created for use by a publisher, and then reproduced into the Steiner published parts. Indeed, a note in Lichtenthal's hand on the Op. 83 score, '*manca la parte del Fagottone*' [this work lacks the contrabassoon] seems specifically intended for the attention of a publisher as the other Krommer partitas all had contrabassoon parts. This sequential difficulty aside, there were other very important considerations about the Milan scores which Blomhert did not address.

First, it is of the utmost significance that the Lichtenthal scores were copied from earlier scores and not copied from individual parts as Blomhert has suggested. In creating a score from parts one begins with some individual part and assigns a reasonable amount of space for the bar, But then, sooner or later, there is a lower voice filled with sixteenth notes for which there is no room in the bar. Here one suddenly sees very small manuscript to squeeze the notes in, or often a special line expanding the bar for that one voice or a N.B. for the bar in the margin, etc. Furthermore, in the new score made from parts the vertical alignment of the notes on the beat never line up because one never knows in advance where that point will be. When copying a score from a score these kinds of problems never exist. One simply cannot be fooled, for it is very obvious whether the copy is being made from an earlier score or from a set of parts. And so the question is, what score was Lichtenthal copying from? The only extant scores at this time were the autograph scores of Krommer. And since *none* of the autograph scores used by Lichtenthal exist today, the potential importance of the Lichtenthal scores might be in their having mirrored the original scores.

It is also important to note, in this regard, that three of the famous Krommer partitas, Op. 71, Op. 73 and Op. 76, partitas for which the earliest manuscript parts are associated together under a single shelf-mark in the National Library in Vienna, are not found in the Milan collection in Lichtenthal's hand. It appears that these particular scores could no longer be produced by Krommer for the purpose of Lichtenthal making presentation copies. Two of the three autograph scores have since turned up, the Op. 71 in Italy and the Op. 73 in Paris. The most reasonable conclusion is that Krommer had earlier made a gift of these three partitas to some interested aristocratic person and felt he could not ask for the scores back to give to Lichtenthal.

The important point is that the remaining seven partita scores in the hand of Lichtenthal may have been made as presentation scores for Steiner, but they were certainly not made from Steiner parts. Lichtenthal was copying from autograph scores, which is where he perhaps unconsciously copied the strange Bass Clef symbol I have mentioned above.

The second very important fact regarding the Milan scores is that they are without Opus numbers. If these scores were copied from Steiner, as Blomhert concluded, or from the earlier published parts by the Chemische Druckerei in Vienna, Lichtenthal would have identified these partitas by their Opus numbers as he went along for the Opus numbers were long since established and known. Indeed, the very creation of the concept of Opus numbers was the work of publishers, not to date a composer's work, but for the publishers to keep track of what they were stealing from each other.

The important point here is that the original Krommer autograph scores had no Opus numbers in his hand. Their following absence in the Milan scores once again associates those scores with the autograph scores.

Taking all this into account I should like to offer the following chronology. There is no question that the first published parts contained numerous errors, due in part to the fact that the laborer was hammering his steel punches for individual notes while looking upside down on a sheet of copper. It was no doubt the frustration of the very fine players in Vienna who raised the plea for newly published parts. Krommer was also no doubt frustrated and I would guess he turned to the young enthusiast of music, Lichtenthal, to help by making presentation scores for future publishers. Since the new Steiner publications appear to be dated ca. 1808–1810, we might assume that Lichtenthal set to work ca. 1806 or so when he would have been twenty-six years of age. As Lichtenthal finished each copy he probably gave the autograph score back to Krommer. On the basis of the one Krommer autograph partita score I have seen, the Op. 71, which is almost as messy as Beethoven manuscripts, Krommer may have elected to throw them away after Lichtenthal had created his presentation scores.

Lichtenthal's presentation scores remained his property and when he moved permanently to Milan in 1810, where he worked as an agent of the Austrian government, they moved with him. In Milan Lichtenthal's passion turned to the music of Mozart and he made numerous arrangements of Mozart's works for string quartet including the G minor *Symphony*, the K.466 piano *Concerto* and the *Requiem*! Why would one want to hear the *Requiem* performed by a string quartet (with no voices)? For the very same reason that *Harmoniemusik* was employed to perform the music of hundreds of different operas at this time. Namely, in an age before the record player, one could hear all those great melodies once again without the cost and complications of bringing into one's private residence a full opera company or orchestra.

*Allegro* (*Harmonie*, Op. 69)
MS  Mss score
  I:Mc (Noseda.M.45.26)

  I:Mc (Da camera 10/6) [later pts]
EP  (Wien:Steiner)
  I:Mc (B.9.h.74)

*Allegro* Op. 79 (*Harmonie*, Op. 67, 79, and 83)
MS  Mss scores
  I:Mc (Noseda.M.45.24)

*Allegro moderato* (Partita)
MS  Mss score
  I:Mc (Noseda.M.45.23)
  This score matches the parts found in BRD:DO, Mus.Ms.1161.

10 *Armonie*
MS  2 volumes of scores
  I:Rsc (G.Mss.32–33)

*Harmonie,* Op. 73
MS
  I:GBc (Mayr.E.2.6)

*Ottetto,* Op. 57
MS  Mss score
  I:Mc (Noseda.M.45.27)

*Nonetto,* Op. 71
MS  Mss score
  I:Mc (Noseaa.Q.31.5)

*Due Ottetti,* Op. 77 (*Harmonies* Op. 77 and 78)
MS  Mss scores
  I:Mc (Noseda.M.45.25)

*Harmonie,* Op. 78
EP  (Wien: Steiner)
  I:Mc (B.9.h.75)

*Parthia* in Dis
MS  pts
  I:OS (Mss.Musiche.B.2242)

*Partita* in E♭
MS  for 22-02
   I:Mc (Da camera MS.12.2)

*Partita*
MS
   I:PAc

*Ottetti* 1-3 (*Harmonies* 57, 77, and 79)
MS  [scores made from parts]
   I:Mc (Da camera Ms.12.1)

*Serenata* in Si bem
MS
   I:Fc (D.V.206) [listed as 14 parts!]

*Sestetto per Armonia*
MS  Mss score
   I:Mc (Noseda.M.45.22)

*Collection* of pieces for band
MS  score
   I:Mc (Noseda Z. 4/17)
   Contains a March in D, 2 Allegretto in G, 2 Allegretto in D, and an Allegretto in
   F, for picoolo, F or G clarinet, 3 C clarinets, bassoons, contrabassoon, serpent, horns,
   trumpets, and percussion.

*Märsche für Türkische Musik*
EP  (Wien, Steiner, Nr. 2807)
   I:MOl [for 222-54, serpent, percussion]

*Trois Marches*, Op. 60
EP  (Wien, Imprimerie Chim., Nr. 1262)
   1:MOl [for 222-12, contrabassoon]
   I:Nc

*Le Dieci Armonie.* Armonia I (only?)
EP  (Firenze:Dallo Stab.Music di Ferd. Lorenzi, sd)
   I:Mc (Part.143/8)

## Lanner, Joseph (1801–1843)

*Drei Märsche des zweiten Wiener Bürger Regimentes*, Op. 157
EP  (London, 1840)
   GB:Lbm (h.861.[11.]) [here for piano]

*Komet-Walzer*, Op. 87
EP   (London, 1880)
      GB:Lbm (h.1549.)

*Kronungs-Galloppe* (1841)
MS   band
      I:OS (Mss.Mus.B.2248)

*Maskenbilder Waltz*
MS   band [arr. Fahrbach]
      I:OS (Mss.Mus.B.1596)

*Die Osmanen*, Valse, Op. 146
EP   (London, 1880)
      GB:Lbm (h.1549.)

*Walzer per banda*
MS
      I:OS (Mss.Mus.B.4850)

*Walzer per banda*
MS
      I:OS (Mss.Mus.B.2249)

## Leonhardt, Andreas (1800–1866)

*Hanoverian*, Quick March
EP   (Londonn, 1858)
      GB:Lbm (h.1562.)

## Neukonun, Sigismund von (1778–1859)

*Three Fanfares* (for four trunpets)
MP   (NewYork, 1965)
      GB:Lbm (g.1110.o.[5.])

*A March & a Gallop March* for a brass band
EP   (London, 1835)
      GB:Lbm (h.723.z.[9.]) [here in a piano arrangement by the composer]

## Nosek, Wenzel

*Fantasie* (ded. K. K. Herrn Ignaz Ritter von Gerhardi)
MS   band
      I:OS (Ms.Mus.B.2441)

**Parlow, Albert (1824–1888)**

*Augusten Polka*, Op. 124
EP  (London, 1882)
    GB:Lbm (h.1549.)

*Damen Galop*, Op. 110
EP  (London, 1871)
    GB:Lbm (h.a544.)

**Sawerthal, Josef (1819–1903)**

*An elegy on the death of the Emperor Maximilian*
EP  (London, 1872)
    GB:Lbn (h.1544.)

**Schubert, Franz (1797–1828)**

[6] *Menuetti* for winds
MP  (Kassel: Bärenreiter, 1970)
    BRD:KA (M.2010)
    US:DW 447

**Seyfried, Ignaz Ritter von (1776–1841)**

*Libera mi Domini*
MS  SATB, 2221-123, tintp (arr. Johann Mayr)
    I:BGc (Fondo Mayr, Faldone 47) [autograph]

Saul König in Israel.
MS (?) 9 winds
    I:BGc (Mayr.E.1.8)

**Strauss, ?**

In distinction to the many contemporary band arrangements of music of the Strauss family, the following works were published in London between 1866–1887, without indication of an arranger.

*Cocorico Polka,* for fife and drum band
    GB:Lbm (f.403.c.[63.])

*The Ladies' Polka*, for fife and drun band
    GB:Lbm (f.403.g.[40.])

*Quick March* in E♭
    GB:Lbm (h.1562.)

## Strauss, Eduard (1835–1916)

In distinction to the many contemporary band arranganents of music of the Strauss family, the following works were published in London between 1871–1897, without indication of an arranger.

*Akademische Burger Valse*, Op. 68
GB:Lbm (h.1544.)

*Alpenrose Polka*, Op. 127
GB:Lbm (h.1549.)

*Carnevals Gruss Mazurka*, Op. 8
GB:Lbm (h.1544.)

*Deutsche Herzen Valse*, Op. 65
GB:Lbm (h.1549.)

*Doctrinen Valses*
GB:Lbm (f.416.[11.])

*Fesche Geister Walzer*, Op. 75
GB:Lbm (h.1562.)
GB:Lbm (f.401.g.[14.])

*Fusionen Valse*, Op. 74
GB:Lbm (h.1544.])
GB:Lbm (f.401.h.[4.])

*Valse Hochzeitslieder*, Op. 290
GB:Lbm (h.1549.)

*Liebeszauber Polka*, Op. 84
GB:Lbm (h.1549.])

*Mit Dampf Galop*, Op. 70
GB:Lbm (h.1549.])

## Strauss, Johann, Jr. (1825–1899)

In distinction to the many contanporaly band arrangements of music of the Strauss family, the following works were published in London between 1860–1889, without indication of an arranger.

*Beautiful Danube Valses*
GB:Lbm (f.412.h.[9.])

*An der schönen blauen Donau Walzer*
GB:Lbm (h.1549.)

*Un Ballo in maschera Quadrille*, Op. 272 (on melodies of Verdi)
GB:Lbm (h.1549.)

*Bei uns z'Haus Valse*
GB:Lbm (h.1549.)

*Cagliostro Valse*, Op. 370
GB:Lbm (h.1549.)

*Carneval's Blider Walzer*
GB:Lbm (h.1549.)

*Carneval's Botschafter Valses*
GB:Lbm (f.415.d.[22.])

*Champagne Polka*, Op. 211
GB:Lbm (h.1544.)

*Conkurrenzen Walzer*, Op. 267
GB:Lbm (h.1544.)

*Figaro Polka*, Op. 320
GB:Lbm (h.1544.)

*Flugschriften Valse*, Op. 300
GB:Lbm (h.1549.)

*Freuet ech des Lebens Walzer*
GB:Lbm (h.1549.)
GB:Lbm (f.416.[13.])

*Die Grillenbanner Walzer*, Op. 247
GB:Lbm (h.1544.)

*Hofballtänze*
GB:Lbm (f.411.c.[21.])

*Immer heiterer Valse*, Op. 235
GB:Lbm (h.1544.)

*Indigo Quadrille*, Op. 344
GB:Lbm (h.1562.)

*Indigo Valse*, Op. 346
GB:Lbm (h.1544.)

*Juristen Ball Tänze*, Op. 177
    GB:Lbm (h.1544.)
    GB:Lbm (f.416.[14.])

*Kolonnen Walzer*, Op. 262
    GB:Lbm (h.1544.)

*Künstler Leben Valse*
    GB:Lbm (h.1549.)
    GB:Lbm (h.1562.)
    GB:Lbm (f.417.[9.])

*Künstler-Quadrille*, Op. 201
    GB:Lbm (h.1549.)

*Lava Ströme Valses*
    GB:Lbm (f.416.[15.])

*Journalisten Valses* (*Die Leitartickel*)
    GB:Lbm (f.411.c.[22.])
    GB:Lbm (h.1544.)

*Leopoldstädter Polka*, Op. 168
    GB:Lbm (h.1549.)

*Nur für Natur Valse*
    GB:Lbm (h.1549.)

*Man lebt nur einmal! Waltzer*, Op. 167
    GB:Lbm (h.1549.)

*Morgenblätter Valses*
    GB:Lbm (f.413.e.[17.])
    GB:Lbm (f.416.[16.])

*Neu Wien Walzer*, Op. 342
    GB:Lbm (h.1544.)
    GB:Lbm (f.416. [17.])

*Neue Melodien Quadrille*, Op. 254
    GB:Lbm (h.1549.)

*Par force Polka*, Op. 308
    GB:Lbm (h.1549.)

*O schöner Mai, Valse*, Op. 375
    GB:Lbm (h.1544.)

*Quadrille, 'Methusalem,'* Op. 376
    GB:Lbm (h.1549.)

*Promotionen Valses*
    GB:Lbm (f.412.h.[13.])

*Sangerlust Polka*, Op. 328
    GB:Lbm (f.414.b.[29.]) [for fife and drum band]

*Die Sanguiniker Valse*
    GB:Lbm (f.401.m.[21.])

*Sans souci Polka*, Op. m78
    GB:Lbm (h.1544.)

*Schall-Wellen Waltzer*, Op. 148
    GB:Lbm (h.1544.)

*Unter Donner und Blitz Polka*
    GB:Lbm (h.1549.)

*Verbrüderungs Marsch*, Op. 287
    GB:Lbm (h.1562.)

*Wein, Weib und Gesang Valses*
    GB:Lbm (h.1562.)
    GB:Lbm (f.416.[19.])

*Wiedersehen Polka*, Op. 142
    GB:Lbm (f.402.d.[34.])
    GB:Lbm (f.414.[93.]) [for fife and drun band]

*Wien, mein Sinn, Walzer*, Op. 192
    GB:Lbm (h.1544.)

*Wiener Bonbons Walzer*, Op. 307
    GB:Lbm (h.1544.)

*Wiener Chronik Walzer*, Op. 268
    GB:Lbm (h.1549.)

*Windsor-Klange Walzer*
    GB:Lbm (f.412.n.[18.])

*Wo die Citronen bluh'n Valse*, Op. 364
    GB:Lbm (h.1549.)

## Strauss, Josef (1827–1870)

In distinction to the many contemporary band arrangements of music of the Strauss family, the following works were published in London between 1859–1886, without indication of an arranger.

*Arm in Arm Polka*, Op. 215
    GB:Lbm (h.1544.)

*Disputationen Valses*, Op. 243
    GB:Lbm (f.416.[12.])

*Eislauf Polka*, Op. 261
    GB:Lbm (h.1549.)

*Die Emancipirte Polka*, Op. 282
    GB:Lbm (h.1544.)

*Gablenz-Marsch*, Op. 159
    GB:Lbm (f.412.h.[11.])
    GB:Lbm (h.1549.)

*The Good old Times Valse*
    GB:Lbm (h.1544.)

*Harold Quadrille*, Op. 157
    GB:Lbm (h.1549.)

*Die Industriellen Walzer*, Op. 158
    GB:Lbm (h.1549.)

*Die Libelle Polka*, Op. 204
    GB:Lbm (h.1544.)

*Liechtenstein March*, Op. 36
    GB:Lbm (h.1562.)

*Moulinet Polka*
    GB:Lbm (f.414.a.[77.])

*Nynphen Polka*, Op. 50
    GB:Lbm (h.1544.)

*Die tanzende Muse Polka*, Op. 266
    GB:Lbm (h.1549.)

*Wiener-Couplets Valses*
    GB:Lbm (f.417.[10.])

*Wiener Kinder Walzer*
GB:Lbm (h.1549.)

*Die Windsbraut Schnell Polka*, Op. 221
GB:Lbm (h.1549.)

## Suppé, Franz von (1819–1895)

*Erzherzog Wilhelm-Marsch*
EP   (Vienna, 1878)
GB:Lbm (h.1570.c.[1.])

*Mannschaft an Bord, Overture*
EP   (London, 1869)
GB:Lbm (h.1544.)

*Morceaux obligato* pour cornet
EP   (London, 1880)
GB:Lbm (h.1549.)

## Wagner, Eduard

*Militar-Messe fur Oesterreichische Militarmusik* (ded: Leone XIII)
MS
I:Rvat (mus.67) [score]

## Ziehrer, Carl Michael (1843–1922)

*Deutsche Lieder Walzer*, Op. 98
EP   (London, 1879)
GB:Lbm (h.1549.)

# Belgium

**Herzeele, F. van**

*Belgian patriotic Fantasia*
EP   (London, 1881)
    GB:Lbm (h.1584.)

*Grand caprice militaire*
EP   (London, 1800)
    GB:Lbm (h.1549.)

*Greeting to England* quick step
EP   (London, 1875)
    GB:Lbm (f.40.c.[9.])

# Denmark

**Lumbye, Hans Christian (1810–1874)**

The following works were published, 1876–1877, in London

*Amelie Valses*
    GB:Lbm (f.416.[8.])

*Esmeralda Schottisch*
    GB:Lbm (f.401.f.[12.])
    GB:Lbm (f.403.c.[44.]) [for fife and drum band]

*Krolls Ball Klange*, valses
    GB:Lbm (f.416.[9.])

*Petersburgh, new Champagne Galop*
    GB:Lbm (f.415.d.[4.])

*Souvenirs de Jenny Lind Valses*
    GB:Lbm (f.416.[10.])

# France

## Arban, J.J. (1825–1889)

*Le Roi Carotte Quadrille*
EP   (London, 1876)
    GB:Lbm (h.1549)

*Les Amazones Volontaires*
EP   (London, 1875)
    GB:Lbm (h.1549.)

## Berlioz, Hector (1803–1869)

*Grande Simphonie*
EP   (Paris, sd)
    I:Mc (A.45.6 .9)

## Bochsa, Charles Nicholas (1789–1856)

*Requiem*
MS   band and chorus
    I:Fc (A.21) [parts]

## Boehlman-Sauzeau, H. (fl. ca. 1820–1850)

*Barbe blue Quadrille*
EP   (London, 1867)
    GB:Lbm (h.1544.)

## Carafa, Michele Enrico (1787–1872)

*Les Adieux. Andante Cantabile* (1846)
MS   solo oboe and band
    I:Nc (III.1.20/6)

*Allegretto giusto* (1851)
MS   solo oboe and band
    I:Nc (III.1.20/6)

*Allegro moderato* (1851)
MS   solo flute and band
    I:Nc (III.1.20/6)

*Andante Cantabile* (1845)
MS  band
    I:Nc (III.1.20/6)

*Armonia*
MS  solo flute, 222-02, ophicleide
    I:Nc (M.S.922-931)

*Harmonie* a 10
MS
    I:Nc (III.1.19/2)

*Marche funèbre* (1846)
MS  band
    I:Nc (III.1.19/2)

*Sicilienne andantino* (1845)
MS  solo horn, band
    I:Nc (III.1.20/6)

*Andante dans l'Ouverture*
MS  trombone and horns
    I:Nc (III.1.20/20)

## Cherubini, Luigi (1760–1842)

*Marcia* (for barone de Braun, 1805)
EP  (Roma, sd)
    I:Mc (A.45.11.18)
MS  I:Ria (Ms.205) [manuscript score copied from the autograph in Berlin]

*Lodoiska*
MS  Harmoniemusik
    I:BGc (Mayr.E.2.19)

## Esch, Louis von

*Marcia* (1839)
MS  band
    I:OS (Mss.Musiche.B.1580/2)

*Passo doppio* (1834)
MS  band
    I:OS (Mss.Musiche.B.1580/1)

## Gebauer, François René (1773–1844)

3 *Quartets* in C, F Minor, A Minor
MS  1011-01
    I:Fc (D.X.114-118)

3 *Quartets* in F, D Minor, G Minor
MS  1011-01
    I:Ria (Ms.629)

## Gotmod, Charles (1818–1893)

*Hymne a St. Cecite*
MS  solo Vln, winds, harp, timp. st.bass
    I:Bc [inc]

## Herman, Alplonse

The following works were published, 1877–1880, in London.

Le Chevalier Breton, Overture, for 'Octet band'.
    GB:Lbm (f.411.a.[27.])

*La Couronne d'Or*, Overture
    GB:Lbm (f.412.c.[26.])
    GB:Lbm (f.411.a.[28.]), for 'octet band'

*Esmeralda*, Overture, for 'octet band'
    GB:Lbm (f.411.a.[29.])

*La Souveraine*, Overture, for 'octet band'
    GB:Lbm (f.411.a.[30.])

*Overture Triomphale*, for 'octet band'
    GB:Llm (f.411.a.[30.])

## Hitz, Franz (1828–1891)

*Sans facon Galop*
EP  (London, 1885)
    GB:Lbm (h.1549.)

## Kastner, Jean Georges (1810–1867)

*Manuel général de musique militarie a l'usage des Armées Françaises.*
EP  (Paris, 1848)
    GB:Lbm (f.173.a.)

*Méthode complète et raisonnée de saxophone.* Dédée à Monsieur Ad. Sax.
EP   (Paris, 1845)
   GB:Lbm (h.2671.)

*Méthode complète et raisonnée de timbales … précédée d'une notice historique*
EP   (Paris, 1840)
   GB:Lbm (f.173.)

*Méthode élémentaire pour la clarinette*
EP   (Paris, 1840)
   GB:Lbm (e.450.)

*Méthode élémentaire pour le cor*
EP   (Paris, 1840)
   GB:Lbm (e.450.a.)

*Méthode élémentaire pour le cornet a pistons*
EP   (Paris, 1840)
   GB:Lbm (e.450.b.)

*Méthode élémentaire pour la flûte*
EP   (Paris, 1850)
   GB:Lbm (e.450.d.)

*Méthode élémentaire pour le hautbois*
EP   (Paris, 1840)
   GB:Lbm (e.450.e.)

*Méthode élémentaire pour l'ophcleide*
EP   (Paris, 1840)
   GB:Lbm (e.450.f.)

*Méthode élémentaire pour le trombone*
EP   (Paris, 1840)
   GB:Lbm (e.450.h.)

## Kling, Henry A. L. (1842–1918)

The following works were published, 1894–1911, in London.

*Le Chemin de la gloire Overture*
   GB:Lbm (h.1544.)

*Écho des Bastions, Caprice*
   GB:Lbm (h.3211.a.[44.])

*Le Flutiste Overture*
   GB:Lbm (h.1544.)

*The Goldbeetles Soirée* (Humorous fantasia)
   GB:Lbm (h.1544.)

*Sacred Fantasia*, 'In the Cathedral'
   GB:Lbm (h.1549.)

*Les Perles, Concert Polka* (xylophone solo)
   GB:Lbm (h.1544.a)

*La Petite marquise* (Pavane for solo cornet)
   GB:Lbm (h.1544.)

*Concerto Polka*, 'Robin and Wren'
   GB:Lbm (h.1549.)

## Klosé, Hyacinthe (1808–1880)

*Artillery galop*
EP   (London, 1877)
   GB:Lbm (f.412.j.[7.])

*The Drummers quick step*
EP   (London, 1880)
   GB:Lbm (f.401.o.[16.])

## Kresser, ?

*Méthode complète pour la Trompette d'Harmonie, suivie d'un notice sur le Cornet*
EP   (Paris, 1850)
   GB:Lbm (h.2317.)

## Laimable, ?

*Le Départ*, quick march
EP   (London, 1879)
   GB:Lbm (f.401.m.[11.])

## Lajarte, Theodore (1826–1890)

*Six Marches* performed by the Garde Républicaine
EP   (London, 1871, as piano duets)
   GB:Lbm (h.1482.y.[20.])

**Lamotte, Nicolas**

The following works were published, 1860–1879, in London.

*La Belle Bordelaise*, grande polka with solo cornet
  GB:Lbm (f.411.b.[8.])

*Les Colombes*, valses
  GB:Lbm (f.413.b.[29.])

*Franklin Polka*
  GB:Lbm (f.411.b.[9.])

*Honey Moon* mazurka
  GB:Lbm (f.414.[36.]), for fife and drum band

*Oreste et Pylade* polka
  GB:Lbm (f.402.c.[21.]), for brass band

*Les Pupilles de la Garde*, Fantaise-march
  GB:Lbm (f.411.b.[10.])

*Queen of Beauty* polka
  GB:Lbm (f.401.c.[27.])
  GB:Lbm (f.403.c.[43.]), for fife and drum band

*Unknown Flower* redowa
  GB:Lbm (f.402.c.[20.]), for brass band

**Latour, Henri**

*Air de Danse*
EP   (London, 1879)
  GB:Lbm (f.401.o.[28])

*Air de Danse*
EP   (London, 1883)
  GB:Lbm (f.401.v.[9.])

**Le Thière, Charles**

The following works were published, 1882–1903, in London.

*Les Alsachinnes, Divertissment* (with solo clarinet)
  GB:Lbm (h.1562.)

*Alanian, Divertissenent* for solo clarinet
  GB:Lbm (h.1544.)

*Amourette, Polka*
    GB:Lbm (f.414.a.[47.])

*Belgravia*, Quick March
    GB:Lbm (f.412.q.[14.])

*Belle Vue*, Fantasia, Op. 110
    GB:Lbm (e.372.f.[1.])

*The Bohemian*, Bolero
    GB:Lbm (f.401.aa.[15.])

*Californian*, Andante and Polonaise (with solo clarinet)
    GB:Lbm (h.1544.)

*Caracalla*, Quick March
    GB:Lbm (f.401.aa.[13.])

*Clarion*, Slow March
    GB:Lbm (e.372.f.[7.])

*Clear the Road*, Galop, Op. 91
    GB:Lbm (e.372.f.[5.])

*Les Cuirassiers*, Galop
    GB:Lbm (f.402.e.[21.]), for brass band

*Danse des aborigènes*
    GB:Lbm (h.1544.)
    GB:Lbm (f.403.f.[38.]), for fife and drum band

*Eclat,* Gavotte
    GB:Lbm (e.372.f.[6.])

*Elka*, Quick March
    GB:Lbm (e.372.f.[9.])

*Fue de Joie*, Galop
    GB:Lbm (f.412.r.[1.])

*Gipsy Life*, Original fantasia
    GB:Lbm (h.1562.)

*Gipsy Queen*, Bolero
    GB:Lbm (f.412.r.[2.])

*The Grenade*, Quick March
    GB:Lbm (e.372.f.[8.])

*Honeymoon Polka*
GB:Lbm (e.372.f.[3.])

*Inesilla*, Quick March
GB:Lbm (e.372.f.[4.])

*Libua March*
GB:Lbm (e.667.c.[1.])

*Love's Adieu*, Valse
GB:Lbm (f.414.b.[21.]), for fife and drum band

*Lucerne*, Quick March
GB:Lbm (f.401.aa.[14.])

*Marche indienne*, Characteristic piece, Op. 160
GB:Lbm (9.1800.[204.])

*The Merry Prince, Polka*, Op. 82
GB:Lbm (e.372.f.[11.])

*Moonlight in the Forest and Dance of the Nynphs*
GB:Lbm (9.1800.[205.])

*Ramleh, Quick March*
GB:Lbm (e.372.f.[2.])

*The Return Home, Quick March*
GB:Lbm (f.412.q.[15.] )

*Roman Life*, Descriptive Fantasia
GB:Lbm (h.1549.)

*Romance & Polacca* (with solo clarinet)
GB:Lbm (h.1549.)

*Roquefort, Quick March*
GB:Lbm (f.800.[817.])

*The Royal Guards, Quick March*
GB:Lbm (e.372.f.[13.])

*Silver Birds, Valse*
GB:Lbm (f.401.ff.[1.])

*Sylvia, Scherzo* (with solo piccolo)
GB:Lbm (g.1800.[207.])

*Theodora, Gavotte* (with solo clarinet)
GB:Lbm (g.1800.[208.])
GB:Lbm (f.414.b.[23.]), for fife and drum band

*The Warrior, Quick March*
GB:Lbm (f.414.b.[24.]), for fife and drum band
GB:Lbm (e.372.f.[12.])

## Ligner, F.

*Ah! vous dirai-je maman*, thème varié
EP (Paris, 1883)
GB:Lbm (f.419.[19.])

*Thème Suisse* varié
EP (Paris, 1883)
GB:Lbm (f.419.[20.])

## Louis, Émile

*Salutation*, Slow March
EP (London, 1887)
GB:Lbm (f.401.ff.[4.])

## Marie, E.

The following works were published, 1873–1887, in London.

*Battle of Magenta* quickstep [for brass band]
GB:Lbm (f.402.c.[24.])

*Beautiful Venice*, barcarole, for brass band
GB:Lbm (f.402.c.[25.])

*The Centurion* quick march
GB:Lbm (f.401.o.[31.])

*The Fifer.* quick step for fife and drum band
GB:Lbm (f.403.a.[32.])

*The First Campaign*, quick step
GB:Lbm (f.401.o.[32.])

*French March*
GB:Lbm (f.401.o.[30.])

*Garland of Flowers* schottische for fife and drum band
    GB:Lbm (f.403.a.[35.])

*La Grande Dame Schottische*, or fife and drl.lll band
    GB:Lbm (f.414.b.[26.])

*A Hunt in the Ardennes*, Overture
    GB:Lbm (f.401.q.[16.])

*Lovely Kett* schottisch for fife and drum band
    GB:Lbm (f.403.c.[47.])

*Magenta* quick step for fife and drum band
    GB:Lbm (f.403.a.[33.])

*Mandolina* bolero for fife and drum band
    GB: Lbm (f.403.c.[48.])

*A New Flower* schottische for brass band
    GB: Lbm (f.402.c.[22.])

*Osman Pasha* quick step
    GB:Lbm (f.401.m.[15.])

*The Pacific*, quick step
    GB:Lbm (f.401.g.[1.])

*La Pergola* polka
    GB:Lbm (f.401.s.[5.])
    GB:Lbm (f.412.d.[1.])
    GB:Lbm (f.415.d.[6.])

*Quick step*, 'Go on' for fife and drum band
    GB:Lbm (f.403.a.[30.])

*The Review* slow march for fife and drum band
    GB:Lbm (f.403.c.[51.])

*Rubis* polka for fife and drum band
    GB:Lbm (f.403.a.[31.])

*Sea Flower* polka
    GB:Lbm (f.401.f.[14.])

*Sevelle*, bolero for brass band
    GB:Lbm (f.402.c.[26.])

*Sham Fight. La Petite Guerre, Overture*
    GB:Lbm (f.401.m.[14.])

*Solferino* slow march
    GB:Lbm (f.402.c.[23.]) for brass band
    GB:Lbm (f.414.a.[49.]) for fife and drum band

*Wimbledon* quadrille
    GB:Lbm (f.401.v.[11.])

*Zephir* galop
    GB:Lbm (f.401.f.[13.])

## Mejo, Guillaune

*Variations sur la chanson*: 'Gaudeamus igitur'
EP    (Leipzig, 1824) [for 1042-033, serpent]
    GB:Lbm (g.474.r.)
MP  www.whitwellbooks.com

## Metra, Olivier (1830–1889)

*La Mascotte*, Quadrille
EP    (London, 1882)
    GB:Lbm (h.1544.)

## Michiels, ?

*Danse de cosaques*, Galop
EP    (London, 1892)
    GB:Lbm (h.1549.)

## Nehr, Émile

*Le Galant Postillon*, slow march
EP    (London, 1877)
    GB:Lbm (f.411.b.[26.])

*Jupiter*, pas redoublé
EP    (London, 1874), for fife and drum band
    GB:Lbm (f.403.a.[40.])

*The Parisian lancers*
EP    (London, 1877)
    GB:Lbm (f.411.b.[27.])

*Polish Lancers* quadrille
EP    (London, 1873), for fife and drum band
    GB:Lbm (f.403.a.[41.])

## Nevaux, Henri

*Divertissement*, 'Doux yeux'
EP   (London, 1890)
   GB:Lbm (h.1549.)

## Parés, Gabriel

*Honneur et patrie*. Marche
MS   band
   I:Ria (MS.129) [autograph]

*Marche des preux*
MS   band
   I:Ria (MS.101)

*Marche tunisienne*
MS   band
   I:Ria (MS.135)

*Le Voltigeur*
MS   band
   I:Ria (MS.105)

## Pessard, Émile Louis Fortune (1843–1917)

*Aubade*, for 1111-01
EP   (Paris, 1880)
   GB:Lbm (f.244.b.[3.])

## Pierne, Henri Constant Gabriel (1863–1937)

*Pastorale*, for 1111-01
EP   (Paris, 1887)
   GB:Lbm (f.244.b.[4.])

*Marche solennelle*, Op. 23, Couronnee au concours de 1889
EP   (Paris, 1889)
   GB:Lbm (f.246.qq.[1.])

## Reicha, Antonin (1770–1836)

*Quintets*
EP   I:Mc (Noseda) [Op. 88, 91, and 99]
MS   I:Mc (Da camera MS 22.4) [Op. 100, Nr. 1, 3, 5]

**Reynaud, Louis**

*Tolosa. Overture Symphonique* pour Fanfare
MS
>  I:Ria (Ms.50)

**Rivière, Jules (1819–1900)**

The following works were published, 1866–1883, in London.

*A. B. C. Free and Easy* quick march
>  GB:Lbm (f.413.d.[4.]), for brass band

*Abyssinian* polka
>  GB:Lbm (f.414.[46.])

*Abyssinian* quick march
>  GB:Lbm (f.412.e.[2.])

*Aesculap* galop
>  GB:Lbm (f.413.f.[19.]), for brass band

*The Aesthetic Valses*
>  GB:Lbm (f.412.n.[16.])

*Air varié* (with solo euphonium)
>  GB:Lbm (f.412.e.[4.])

*Alexandrowna* quick march
>  GB:Lbm (f.415.a.[8.])

*The Alhambra* quadrille
>  GB:Lbm (f.412.e.[5.])
>  GB:Lbm (f.414.[48.]), for fife and drum band

*All the Rage*, quick march
>  GB:Lbm (f.412.e.[6.])

*The Almees* mazurka
>  GB:Lbm (f.412.e.[7.])

*Anglo-Russian* quick march
>  GB:Lbm (f.412.e.[8.])

*Arcadia* quick march
>  GB:Lbm (f.414.[49.]), for fife and drum band

*Auricomus* quick march
>  GB:Lbm (f.418.[19.]), for bugle band

*Autumn Manoeuvres* pas redoublé
     GB:Lbm (f.412.e.[9.])

*Babil and Bijou* fantasia
     GB:Lbm (f.414.[50.]), for fife and drum band

*Babil & Bijou* quadrille
     GB:Lbm (f.412.e.[10.])

*Bacchus Cortege* quick march
     GB:Lbm (f.412.e.[11.])

*Bagatelle* mazurka
     GB:Lbm (f.412.j.[12.])

*The Bayadere* quick march
     GB:Lbm (f.414.[51.]), for fife and drum band

*Beautiful Flowers* valses
     GB:Lbm (f.412.e.[12.])

*Beautiful for Ever* quick march
     GB:Lbm (f.413.c.[14.]), for brass band

*Beautiful Isle of the Sea*, fantasia
     GB:Lbm (f.413.c.[15.]), for brass band

*La Belle France*, pas redoublé
     GB:Lbm (f.412.e.[13.])

*The Bird on the Tree,* quick march
     GB:Lbm (f.413.c.[17.]), for brass band

*The Black Crook*, pas redoublé
     GB:Lbm (f.412.e.[14.])

*The Black Watch*, quick march
     GB:Lbm (f.412.e.[15.])

*The Blind Boy*, quick march
     GB:Lbm (f.414.a.[66.]), for fife and drum band

*Bouquet d'Opera* comique quadrille
     GB:Lbm (f.412.e.[17.])

*La Brabanconne* slow march
     GB:Lbm (f.414. [52.]), for fife and drum band

*Brigade* troop
     GB:Lbm (f.412.e.[18.])

*The Brighton Boatman*, quick march
  GB:Lbm (f.413.c.[18.]), for brass band

*The British Army* grand pas redoublé from Jullien's quadrille
  GB:Lbm (f.412.e.[19.])

*Calypso* shottische
  GB:Lbm (f.412.e.[20.])
  GB:Lbm (f.414.[53.]), for fife and drum band

*Cambrian* quick march
  GB:Lbm (f.414.a.[57.]), for fife and drum band

*Captain Jinks* quick march
  GB:Lbm (f.412.e.[21.])

*Carlotta*, set of valses
  GB:Lbm (f.411.c.[2.])

*Catalonia* bolero
  GB:Lbm (f.414.[54.]), for fife and drum band

*Cérès redowa*
  GB:Lbm (f.412.e.[22.])

*Cherry Ripe*. Quick march
  GB:Lbm (f.414.a.[67.]), for fife and drum band

*Circaussian* quick march
  GB:Lbm (f.418.[20.]), for bugle band

*Clicquot* galop
  GB:Lbm (f.415.b.[8.])

*Collodion* galop
  GB:Lbm (f.414.[55.]), for fife and drum band

*Corricolo* quick march
  GB:Lbm (f.414.[56.], for fife and drum band

*Covent Garden* polka
  GB:Lbm (f.414.[57.]), for fife and drum band

*Croquefer* quick march
  GB:Lbm (f.414.[58.]), for fife and drum band

*Dear England*, pas redoublé
  GB:Lbm (f.412.e.[26.])

*Dejazet* quadrille
GB:Lbm (f.413.c.[20.]), for brass band

*Don Quixote* quick march
GB:Lbm (f.418.[21.]), for bugle band
GB:Lbm (f.414.a.[61.]), for fife and drum band

*Dorkin's Night* quick march
GB:Lbm (f.413.f.[13.]), for brass band

*Dragonette* quick march
GB:Lbm (f.414.a.[72.]) [for fife and drum band]

*The Dutchman's Wee Dog* quick march
GB:Lbm (f.414.[59.]), for fife and drum band

*Echoes of the Night*, grand serio-comic fantasia
GB:Lbm (f.413.c.[21.]), for brass band

*Excelsior* quick march
GB:Lbm (f.412.f.[2.])

*Exile and return* (with soli cornet and euponiun)
GB:Lbm (f.402.e.[27.]), for brass band

*Fair Rosabelle* serenade
GB:Lbm (f.413.c.[22.]), for brass band

*Fairy Bells* galop
GB:Lbm (f.414.[62.]), for fife and drum band

*Fancy* quick march
GB:Lbm (f.414.[61.]), for fife and drum band

*Fantistcuff* quick march
GB:Lbm (f.414.[60.]), for fife and drum band

*Fashionable schottische*
GB:Lbm (f.412.f.[6.])

*Father, come home*, quick march
GB:Lbm (f.412.f.[7.])

*La Fille du Regiment* pas redoublé
GB:Lbm (f.412.f.[8.])

*Flamma pas redoublé*
GB:Lbm (f.412.f.[10.])

*Flamna. La Pitteri* set of valses
GB:Lbm (f.412.g.[4.])

*Les Fleurs du Nord*, fantaisie sur des airs Russes
GB:Lbm (f.413.c.[24.]), for brass band
GB:Lbm (f.411.c.[4.])

*Fortunio* quick march
GB:Lbm (f.414.[63.]), for fife and drum band

*The Foundry* galop
GB:Lbm (f.402.d.[10]), for brass band

*The Gaiety* quick march
GB:Lbm (f.412.f.[11.])

*Le Gaulois*, pas redoublé
GB:Lbm (f.412.n.[14.])

*Gladiateur* quick march
GB:Lbm (f.412.f.[14.])

*Glockenspiel* quick march
GB:Lbm (f.412.f.[15.])

*God bless Victoria's Sons*, quick march
GB:Lbm (f.413.d.[6.]), for brass band

*Goliath* quick march
GB:Lbm (f.412.f.[16.])

*The Grecian Bend* quick march
GB:Lbm (f.413.d.[7.]). for brass band

*Health to the Bride*, quick march
GB:Lbm (f.412.f.[17.])

*He was a careful man.* Quick march
GB:Lbm (f.414.a.[73.]), for fife and drum band

*Herculean, Trombone Polka*
GB:Lbm (f.411.c.[6.])

*Honduras* quick march
GB:Lbm (f.414.[66.]), for fife and drum band

*Hunkey Dorum* quick march
GB:Lbm (f.412.f.[18.])

*The Hunters* quick march
    GB:Ltm (f.418.[23.]), for bugle band

*Hurrah! Hurrah!* quick march
    GB:Lbm (f.412.f.[19.])

*I won her heart*, quick march
    GB:Lbm (f.418.[24.]), for bugle band

*Imnensikuff* quick march
    GB:Lbm (f.412.f.[20.])

*In the South*, quick march
    GB:Lbm (f.414.[67.]), for fife and drum band

*International* quick march
    GB:Lbm (f.412.f.[21.])

*It's naughty but it's nice*, quick march
    GB:Lbm (f.414.[68.]), for fife and drum band

*Italian Bouquet* set of valses
    GB:Lbm (f.412.f.[23.])

*Jack the Dandy* quick march
    GB:Lbm (f.414.[69.]), for fife and drum band

*John Brown* quick march
    GB:Lbm (f.412.f.[22.])

*Killarney*. quick march
    GB:Lbm (f.402.e.[28.]), for brass band

*The Lancashire Lass* quick march
    GB:Lbm (f.413.d.[8.]), for brass band

*Little Emily* quick march
    GB:Lbm (f.413.f.[21.])

*The Little Empty Cradle* quick march
    GB:Lbm (f.413.f.[21.])

*Little Katie's sorrow*. Quick march
    GB:Lbm (f.414.a.[71.]), for fife and drum band

*Little Maggie May* quick march
    GB:Lbm (f.414.[70.]), for fife and drum band

*Love Letter* polka
    GB:Lbm (f.413.d.[11.]), for brass band

*The Lover and the Bird* fantasia
GB:Lbm (f.413.d.[12.]), for brass band

*Lullaby* Quick march
GB:Lbm (f.413.d.[13.]), for brass band

*Ma Lisette*, pas redoublé
GB:Lbm (f.412.f.[29.])

*Magdala* quick march
GB:Lbm (f.414.[71.]), for fife and drum band

*Mandolinata* quick march
GB:Lbm (f.412.f.[30.])

*March of the Period* quick march
GB:Lbm (f.412.f.[31.])

*Maritana* quick march
GB:Lbm (f.412.f.[32.])

*May Blossams* valses
GB:Lbm (f.414.[73.]), for fife and drum band

*Meet me Josie* quick march
GB:Lbm (f.413.d.[14.]), for brass band

*Miss Wobbington,* quick march
GB:Lbn (f.418.[25.]), for bugle band

*Montenegro* quick march
GB:Lbn (f.412.f.[33.])

*Monthabor* quick march
GB:Lbm (f.413.f.[16.]), for brass band

*Morning Breezes* fantasia
GB:Lbm (f.413.d.[15.]), for brass band

*Mosaic*, grand air varié
GB:Lbm (f.411.c.[5.])

*Mosquita* mazurka
GB:Lbm (f.413.d.[16.]), for brass band

*A Motto for every Man* quick march
GB:Lbm (f.413.d.[17.]), for brass band

*Les Mousquetaires* mazurka
GB:Lbm (f.412.n.[15.])

*Les Mousquetaires* valses
GB:Lbm (f.413.f.[18.]), for brass band

*The Mulligan Guards* quick march
GB:Lbm (f.412.f.[34.])

*Musical Review*, Serio-comic fantasia
GB:Lbm (f.412.1.[19.])

*Mustapha Pacha* quick march
GB:Lbm (f.413.d.[18.]), for brass band

*Nautilus* quick march
GB:Lbm (f.418.[26.]), for bugle band

*The New Christy's Minstrels* quick march
GB:Lbm (f.412.f.[35.])

*Not for Joseph* quick march
GB:Lbm (f.414.[74.]), for fife and drum band

*Ocean* galop
GB:Lbm (f.414.[75.]), for fife and drum band

*Oh! dem golden slippers.* Quick march
GB:Lbm (f.414.a.[74.]), for fife and drum band

*Oh! would I were a bird*, quick march
GB:Lbm (f.414.[77.]), for fife and drum band

*Oriental* pas redoublé
GB:Lbm (f.412.g.[2.])

*The Pages* quick march
GB:Lbm (f.413.d.[19.]), for brass band

*Pegase* galop
GB:Lbm (f.418.[27.]), for bugle band

*Pepito* schottische
GB:Lbm (f.401.b.[16.])

*Phoenix* slow rrarch
GB:Lbm (f.412.g.[3.])

*Les Pompiers de France* quadrille
GB:Lbm (f.413.d.[20.]), for brass band

*Les Panpiers de France* quick march
GB:Lbm (f.413.d.[21.]), for brass band

*Les Pompiers de Nanterre* quadrille
   GB:Lbm (f.414.a.[64.]), for fife and drum band

*Pongo* galop
   GB:Lbm (f.418.[28.]), for bugle band

*Pretty Jemima* quick march
   GB:Lbm (f.413.d.[22.]), for brass band

*Princess Fortinbras* quick march
   GB:Lbm (f.412.g.[6.])

*Princess Toto* quick march
   GB:Lbm (f.412.j.[10.])

*Queen Mab* quick march
   GB:Lbm (f.418. [78.]), for bugle band

*Quicksilver* galop
   GB:Lbm (f.414.[78.]), for fife and drum band

*Ra-fla-fla-* polka
   GB:Lbm (f.412.k.[14.])

*The Ranelagh* polka
   GB:Lbm (f.411.c.[9.])

*Rigolo* quick march
   GB:Lbm (f.414.[79.]), for fife and drum band

*The Rollicking Rams* quick march
   GB:Lbm (f.413.d.[25.]), for brass band

*The Roman Fall* quick march
   GB:Lbm (f.413.d. [26.]), for brass band

*Les Roses* quick march
   GB:Lbm (f.413.d.[27]), for brass band

*Royal Irish* quadrille
   GB:Lbm (f.413.d.[28.]), for brass band

*Russian* quadrille
   GB:Lbm (f.413.d.[29.]), for brass band

*Rustic* polka
   GB:Lbm (f.414.[81.]), for fife and drum band

*St. Malo* quick march
   GB:Lbm (f.413.d.[30.]), for brass band

*Salamanca* bolero
　　GB:Lbm (f.412.g.[8.])
　　GB:Lbm (f.411.c.[10.])

*Salisbury* slow march
　　GB:Lbm (f.418.[31.]), for bugle band

*The Scamp* quick march
　　GB:Lbm (f.413.d.[31.])

*Sea Nymphs* galop
　　GB:Lbm (f.412.k.[15.])

*Sentinentale redowa*
　　GB:Lbm (f.413.f.[17.]), for brass band

*A Set of Country Dances*
　　GB:Lbm (f.412.g.[9.])

*A Set of four Songs*
　　GB:Lbm (f.412.g.[10.])

*3rd Set of National Melodies*
　　GB:Lbm (f.412.g.[10.])

*Should he upbraid,* quick march
　　GB:Lbm (f.414.[82.]), for fife and drum band

*Shoulder to shoulder* march
　　GB:Lbm (f.402.e.[24.]), for brass band

*Silver Thread among the Gold,* quick march
　　GB:Lbm (f.413.d.[32.]), for brass band
　　GB:Lbm (f.414.[83.]) [for fife and drum band

*Sing, birdie, sing,* quick march
　　GB:Lbm (f.412.g.[12.])

*Sly Young Coon* quick march
　　GB:Lbm (f.418.[32.]), for bugle band

*The Song of the Regiment,* pas redoublé
　　GB:Lbm (f.413.d.[33.]), for brass band

*Spanish Bouquet* quadrille
　　GB:Lbm (f.413.d.[34.]), for brass band

*Spring* quick march
　　GB:Lbm (f.413.e.[1.]), for brass band

*Starry Night for a Ramble*, quick march
GB:Lbm (f.414.[84.]), for fife and drum band

*The Sultan of Mocha*, quick march
GB:Lbm (f.412.g.[14.])

*Sunlight Quick March*
GB:Lbm (f.402.e.[26.]), for brass band

*Superba* quick march
GB:Lbm (f.412.g.[15.])

*Tambour Major* pas redoublé
GB:Lbm (f.412.g.[15.])

*Ten Little Niggers*, quick march
GB:Lbm (f.412.g. [16.]), for fife and drum band

*Thimble Jack Polka*
GB:Lbm (f.414.a.[85.]), for fife and drum band

*The Three young men of Ware.* Quick march
GB:Lbm (f.402.e.[25.]), for brass band

*Tomahawk* quick march
GB:Lbm (f.413.e.[3.]), for brass band

*Tommy Dodd* quick march
GB:Lbm (f.413.e.[4.1]), for brass band

*Tommy make room for your Uncle* quick march
GB:Lbm (f.413.e.[5.]), for brass band
GB:Lbm (f.414.[86.]), for fife and drum band

*Tramp, Tramp*, quick march
GB:Lbm (f.412.g.[17.])
GB:Lbm (f.414.[87.]), for fife and drum band

*Tullochgorum* quadrille
GB:Lbm (f.413.e.[6.]), for brass band

*Tyrolean Echos Serenade*
GB:Lbm (f.412.g.[18.])
GB:Lbm (f.411.c.[11.])

*The United Service* serio-comic fantasia
GB:Lbm (f.413.e.[7.]), for brass band

*Up in a Balloon* quick march
    GB:Lbm (f.412.g.[19.])

*U-pi-dee* quick march
    GB:Lbm (f.413.e.[18.]), for brass band

*Victoria* quick march
    GB:Lbm (f.413.e.[9.]), for brass band
    GB:Lbm (f.411.c.[12.])

*Viva Verdi* galop
    GB:Lbm (f.402.d.[9.]), for brass band
    GB:Lbm (f.414.a.[65.]), for fife and drum band

*War Songs of France and Germany*
    GB:Lbm (f.412.g.[20.])

*Widow Macree Quick March*
    GB:Lbm (f.414.a.[58.]), for fife and drun band

*Winter Garden* quadrille
    GB:Lbm (f.412.n.[17.])

*The Woolwich Infant* quick march
    GB:Lbm (f.412.g.[21.])

*Zulika* polonaise
    GB:Lbm (f.402.d.[13.]), for brass band

*Riviere and Hawkes Excelsior grand military band journal*
    GB:Lbm (h.1563.)

## Saint-Saëns, Camille (1835–1921)

*Orient & Occident*, grande marche
EP   (Paris, 1881)
    GB:Lbm (h.1509.i.[5.])
MP   www.whitwellbooks.com

*Henry VIII*. Fantasia per Banda
MS
    I:Ria (Ms.125)

*Suite Algerienne*
MS   band
    I:Mscala ('18 batt.ms.auto')

*Sur les Bords du Nile*
MS  band
    I:Rasc [arr. by Vessella]
MP  US:DW (1391) [Modern edition]

## Signard, P.

The following were published, 1878–1884, in Paris.

*Hanoï*, Pas redoublé
    GB:Lbm (e.666.g.[27.])

*Marchons au Pas!* pas redoublé
    GB:Lbm (f.244.a.[6.])

*La Sainte Cécile*, quadrille
    GB:Lbm (f.419.[31.])

*Serrons nos Rangs!!* pas redoublé
    GB:Lbm (f.244.a.[7.])

## Sohier, Henri

*Le Premier soldat d'Italie.* Pas redoublé
MS  band
    I:Tr (Ob. 209)

*Retraite Franco-Piemontaise*
MS  band
    I:Tr (Ob. 294)

## Tollot, J.

The following works were published, 1873–1881, in London.

*The Broken Head* quick step
    GB:Lbm (f.403.c.[66.])

*Dulcigno* quick step
    GB:Lbm (f.401.r.[24.])

*Evening Breeze* valses
    GB:Lbm (f.403.b. [42.]), for fife and drum band

*Irresistible Valses*
    GB:Lbm (f.402.e.[32.]), for brass band

*The Peace* slow march
    GB:Lbm (f.403.b.[41.]), for fife and drum band

*Le 49me Bataillon* pas redoublé
    GB:Lbm (f.403.b.[40.]), for fife and drum band

## Vern, Auguste

*Nocturne* en harmonie in F (7 movements)
MS   1222-121, serpent
    I:Ria (Ms.267)

## Walckiers, Eugene (1793–1866)

*Cinquiene quatuor* in ut mineur
EP   (Paris, Brandus, 1850, for 1011-01)
    GB:Lbm (h.2801.aa.[1.])

## Waldteufel, Émile (1837–1915)

The following works were published in London, 1877–1904.

*A toi, Valse*, Op. 150
    GB:Lbm (h.1544)

*Acclamations, Valse*, Op. 223
    GB:Lbm (h.1544.)

*Amitié, Valse*
    GB:Lbm (h.1544.)

*Bagatelle, Polka*
    GB:Lbm (h.1549.)

*La Barcarolle, Valse*
    GB:Lbm (h.1549.)

*Les Bohemiens, Polka*
    GB:Lbm (h.1549.)

*Bonne Bouche, Polka*
    GB:Lbm (f.412.1.[24.])

*Camarade, Polka*
    GB:Lbm (h.1549.)

*Chantilly, Valse*, Op. 171
    GB:Lbm (h.1544.)

*Douce souvenance, Valse*
  GB:Lbm (h.1549.)

*En Garde, Polka*
  GB:Lbm (h.1549.)

*Entre nous, Valse*
  GB:Lbm (h.1549.)

*L'Esprit francais, Polka*
  GB:Lbm (h.1549.)

*Etincellse, Valse*, Op. 229
  GB:Lbm (h.1544.)

*L'Etoile Polaire, Valse*
  GB:Lbm (h.1549.)

*The Grenadiers. Valse militaire*
  GB:Lbm (h.1562.)

*Jeunesse Doree Valse*
  GB:Lbm (h.1549.)

*Lune de miel, Valse,*
  GB:Lbm (h.1549.)

*Ma charmante, Valse*
  GB:Lbm (h.1548.)

*Manolo Walzer*
  GB:Lbm (h.1549.)

*Mello*, set of valses
  GB:Lbm (f.412.h.[19.])

*Minuit Polka*
  GB:Lbm (h.1549.)

*Naples, Valse*
  GB:Lbm (h.1544.)

*Pomone Valse*
  GB:Lbm (h.1549.)

*Les Patineurs, Valse*
  GB:Lbm (h.1549.)

*Un Premiere bouquet, Valse*
    GB:Lbm (h.1549)

*La Reine des coeurs, Valse*
    GB:Lbm (h.1549.)

*Rêverie, Valse*
    GB:Lbm (h.1549.)

*Roses de Noël, Valse*
    GB:Lbm (h.1549.)

*Sentiers fleuris, Valse*, Op. 186
    GB:Lbm (h.1544.)

*Soirée d'Été*, Op. 188
    GB:Lbm (h.1544.)

*Souviens toi, Valse*, Op. *173*
    GB:Lbm (h.1544.)

*Sur la plage, Valse*, Op. 234
    GB:Lbm (h.1544.)

*Tendres baisers, Valse*, Op. 211
    GB:Lbm (h.1544.)

*Tendresse, Valse*, Op. 217
    GB:Lbm (h.1544.)

*Violettes*, Valse
    GB:Lbm (h.1544.)

*Vision, Valse*
    GB:Lbm (h.1549.)

## Waterson, James

The following works were published in London, 1865–1886.

*Autumn Manoieuvres*, Pas redoublé
    GB:Lbm (h.1562.)

*Le Cortège des Muses March*
    GB:Lbm (f.412.h.[21.])

*Egypt Grand March*
    GB:Lbm (f.412.r.[18.])

*Farewell* pas redoublé
  GB:Lbm (f.412.1.[25.])

*Ferozeshah* pas redoublé
  GB:Lbm (f.412.h.[22.])

*Grand quartett* (for four clarinets)
  GB:Lbm (h.2189.g.[11.])

*The Merry Bell* galop
  GB:Lbm (f.412.j.[14.])

*Military Overture*, 'Fest'
  GB:Lbm (h.1562.)

*Nora Creina March*
  GB:Lbm (f.412.h.[23.])

*Old Jack Salt March*
  GB:Lbm (f.401.s.[14.])

*Quintet* in F, for 1111-01
  GB:Lbm (g.417.1.[3.])

*Grand Triumphal March*
  GB:Lbm (h.1562.)

*The Troopers' Galop*
  GB:Lbm (h.1562.)

# Germany

**Collections:**

*1834 Inventory of Kgl. Hoftheater in Stuttgart*
BRD:Sl (H.B.XVII, Nr. 940)
This catalog lists Harmoniemusik works by Tausch, Krommer, Pleyel, Mozart, Stumpf, *Jean de Paris* arr. by Kechtler, a work by Legrand, *Septetti* by Beethoven, *Variations* Op. 40 by Rumel, *Septet* by Winter, and original works and arrangements by Schwegler for 2222-22, timp.

28 *Märsche* für Orchestra oder Klavier (1870-1917)
MS  ?, BRD:Sl (H.B.XVII, Nr. 908) This collection includes:
Nr. 4 Wiese, Fr. *Wüttembergischer Siegesmarch*
Nr. 5 Komzak. *König Karl Marsch*
Nr. 8 Auberlen, Louis. *Deutscher Einigungs Marsch*
Nr. 11 Klein, B. *Hell Wüttemberg Marsch*
Nr. 15 Machtle, Adolf. *König Wilhelm Marsch*, Op. 33
Nr. 17 Kohn, Andreas. *Marsch* [Nr. 27, same for cavalry]
Nr. 18 Loeb, Wilhelm. *Jubilemus Hymne*
Nr. 24 Sander, Otto. *Jubilämus Marsch*

*Märsche*. Lieferung XIV
EP  (Hannover: Oertel, 1885–1887)
GB:Lbm (c.120.a. [2.]) [missing all but Cornetto I]

*Sammlung von Märschen für Militair-Musik*, No. 196–200
EP  (Berlin, 1867–1868)
GB:Lbm (h.3213.1.[9.])

Sechs *Märschen fur das gesammte Burgennilitar des Königreichs Baiern*
EP  (Germany, 1807)
GB:Lbm (Hirsch III.544.)

*Sammlung von Märschen für Türkische Musik* zum bestimmten Gebrauch der königlich preussischen Armee. Geschwinder Schritt. Hft. 3
EP  (Berlin: Schlesinger, 1818)
GB:Lbm (g.847.a.)

**Anonymous**

*Prasentinnarsch der Kaiserlich Deutschen Marine*
EP   (Leipzig, 1901)
    GB:Lbm (f.244.e.[2.])

Collection of 85 *'militari e altri pezzi'*
MS   band
    I:Ma (S.122.inf.) [may be the repertoire of a German band in Italy]

**Abert, Johann Joseph (1832–1915)**

*Der 100 Psalm* (1881)
MS   TTBB, -2211
    BRD:S1 (cod.nus.II.fol; Abert Nachlass, Nr. 4)

**Albert, Charles d' (1864–1932)**

*Deer-Dropp Valzer*
MS   band
    I:FEM

**Bärmann, Heinrich Joseph (1784–1847)**

*Concertino* in C (1865)
MS   Clarinet and band
    I:Ria (Ms. 279)

**Bülow, Hans G. von (1830–1894)**

*Humoristische Quadrille*
EP   (London, 1880)
    GB:Lbm (h.1544.)

**Coenen, Johannes (1824–1899)**

*Ein schöner frülingstag* (*Tongemalde für Harmoniemusik*, ca. 1860)
MS   band
    BRD:Sl (H.B.XVII, Nr. 924)

**Curschmann, Karl Friedrich (1804–1841)**

*Lied* [for band]
EP   (London, 1877)
    GB:Lbm (h.1544.)

## Doppler, ?

*Ohne Rast und ohne Ruh Galop*
EP   (London, 1880)
   GB:Lbm (h.1549.)

## Faisst, Immanuel (1823–1894)

*Schiller-Cantate*, Op. 31 (1876)
MS   TBB, cavalry band
   BRD:Sl (cod.mus.II.fol., Nr. 158.a.b.)

*Das 117th Psalm*, 1855
MS   TTBB, cavalry band
   BRD:Sl (cod.mus.II.fol., Nr. 144)

## Gumbert, Friedrich (1841–1906)

*O bitt' euch liebe Vogelein*
EP   (London, 1880)
   GB:Lbm (h.1549.)

## Heinsdorff, G. von

*A. B. C. polka*, for brass band
EP   (London, 1873)
   GB:Lbm (f.402.c.[8.])

## Herchenröder, ?

*Selenen Polka*
EP   (London, 1858)
   GB:Lbm (h.1544.)

*Strohfiedel Galopp*
EP   (London, 1859)
   GB:Lbm (h.1544.)

## Herfurth, ?

*Marien Quadrille*
EP   (London, 1874)
   GB:Lbm (h.1549.)

**Herfurth, w.**

*Abschieds Stänchen*, Op. 85
EP   (London, 1878)
      GB:Lbm (h.1549.)

**Hermann, ?**

*Mythenfest Polka*
EP   (London, 1866)
      GB:Lbm (h.1544.)

**Hertel, Peter Ludwig (1817–1899)**

The following works were published, 1870–1886, in London.

*Fantasca Quadrille*
      GB:Lbm (h.1549.)

*Flick and Flock Galop*
      GB:Lbm (h.1549.)

*Husaren Polka*, Op. 103
      GB:Lbm (h.1544.)

*Morgano Ouadrille*
      GB:Lbm (h.1549.)

*Ulanen Galop*, Op. 100
      GB:Lbm (h.lS44.)

**Hertl, ?**

*March Amazonen*
EP   (London, 1872)
      GB:Lbm (h.1562.)

**Hilge, W. G.**

*Die Leibgarde* (Quick March)
EP   (Lonlon, 1893)
      GB:Lbm (h.1544.)

**Hofmann, Heinrich Karl Johann (1842–1902)**

*Aennchen von Tharau*, Fest Marsch
EP   (London, 1896)
      GB:Lbm (h.1544.)

## Horn, August

*Des Sängers Welt*
EP   (Leipzig, 1879) [Male chorus and five brass instruments]
    GB:Lbm (H.1781.g.[20.])

## Isenmann, Carl

*Lobgesang,* Op. 107, for male chorus, and -331, timpani.
EP   (Leipzig, 1887)
    GB:Lbm (E.308.r.[15.])

## Jacobi, Georg (1840–1906)

*Polish Lancers Galop*
EP   (London, 1885)
    GB:Lbm (f.412.q.[8.])

## Kaernpfert, Max (1871–1941)

*Altschwäbisher Hallorenmarsch*, ca. 1899
MS   band
    BRD:Sl (H.B.XVII, Nr. 923.a)

## Kiefert, Carl (1855–1937)

*The French Maid, Valse*
EP   (London, 1898)
    GB:Lbm (h.1544.)

## Kluhs, Th.

*Gavotte, Willkommen*
EP   (London, 1884)
    GB:Lbm (h.1549.)

## Knobloch, ?

*Amorspfeil, Polka*
EP   (London, 1879)
    GB:Lbm (h.1549.)

## Kücken, Friedrich Wilhelm (1810–1882)

*Die Flucht nach der Schweiz Overture*
EP   (London, 1876)
   GB:Lbm (h.1549.)

## Küffner, Josef (1776–1856)

10 *Trompetten-Aufzüge* … für militar Musik
EP   (Offenbach, 1815)
   GB:Lbm (f.246.e.[4.])

*Musik Mil.*, Op. 146
MS   band
   I:Ria (Ms.274)

*Musique turque.* 9. Recueil [7 compositions]
MS   band
   I:Ria (Ms.313)

*Musique turque.* 10-13 Recueil
MS   band
   I:Ria (Ms.350)

## Kühner, Wilhelm

The following works were published in London, 1851–1889.

*Paul, Mazurka*
   GB:Lbm (h.1544.)

*Anna, Mazurka*
   GB:Lbm (h.1544.)

*Californian Galop*
   GB:Lbm (h.1544.)

*Commerce, Quadrille* on German university songs
   GB:Lbm (h.1544.)

*Eliten March*
   GB:Lbm (h.1549.)

*Emma Walzer*
   GB:Lbm (h.1544.)

*Die Enz Flosser Galop,* Op. 159
   GB:Lbm (h.1544.)

*Fest Polonaise*
    GB:Lbm (h.1544.)

*Forward, Galop*
    GB:Lbm (h.1549.)

*Frankfurter Palmengarten, Quadrille*
    GB:Lbm (h.1549.)

*Friedens Jubel Galop*
    GB:Lbm (h.1549)

*Greeting to London Polka-mazurka*
    GB:Lbm (h.1549.)

*Hannah, Polka* (glockenspiel solo)
    GB:Lbm (h.1544.)

*Klange aus dem Schwarzenwald* (Redowa)
    GB:Lbm (h.1544.)

*Klumpp March*
    GB:Lbm (h.1562.)

*Künstler Potpourri*
    GB:Lbm (h.1549.)

*Der Luftschiffer Polka,* Op. 136
    GB:Lbm (h.1549.)

*Marlow Polka*
    GB:Lbm (h.1549.)

*Mathieux Polka-mazurka*
    GB:Lbm (h.1549)

*Maximilian Galopp*
    GB:Lbm (h.1544.)

*Melanie, Polka-mazurka*
    GB:Lbm (h.1544)

*Minstrel's Songs, Quadrille*
    GB:Lbm (h.1544.)

*Otto, Galop*
    GB:Lbm (h.1544.)

*Pepita Oliva Polka*
  GB:Lbm (h.1544.)

*A Phantom, Mazurka*
  GB:Lbm (h.1544.)

*Politechniker Galop*
  GB:Lbm (h.1549.)

*Rosa Valse or Troop*
  GB:Lbm (h.1549.)

*Sleigh Galop*
  GB:Lbm (h.1544.)

*Stradella, Polonaise*
  GB:Lbm (h.1544.)

*Stuttgarter Königsbau Galop*
  GB:Lbm (h.1544.)

*Les Vepres sicliennes Quadrille*
  GB:Lbm (h.1544.)
  Based on Verdi's *Sicilian Vespers*.

*Verlobungs Galop*
  GB:Lbm (h.1544.)

*Victoria Galop*
  GB:Lbm (h.1544.)

*Wildbad Eisenbahn Galop*
  GB:Lbm (h.1549.)

*Wildbader Colonnaden March*
  GB:Lbm (h.1549.)

## Labitsky, Josef (1802–1881)

*Leinat's Klaenge Valse*
  EP (London, 1876)
  GB:Lbm (h.1544)

*Podagra Polka*
  EP (London, 1879)
  GB:Lbm (h.1549.)

## Lachner, Franz (1803–1890)

*Octett*
EP (Leipzig: Kistner, 1872)
    BRD:KA (M 1201.R.1)
    GB:Lbm (e.66.b.)

*Nonett*, for 2 trumpets, 4 horns, and 3 trombones
MP (Leipzig: Hofneister, 1955)
    GB:Lbm (g.417.vv.[2.])

## Lachner, Vinzenz (1811–1893)

*Marsch-Overture*, Op. 54
MS band
    I:Ria (Ms.241)

## Landsberg, Ludwig (1807–1858)

*Novena cantata* dai Pifferari e accompagnata dalla loro Cornamusa ... messa in musica per
    Piano e canto ad libitum
EP (Rome, 1850)
    GB:Lbm (G.424.c.[3.])

## Lange, Gustav (1830–1889)

The following works were published, 1876–1905, in London.

*Die Sennerin* (Swiss idyll), Op. 63
    GB:Lbm (h.1544.a)

*An der Wiege*, Cradle Song
    GB:Lbm (h.1544.)

*Blumen am Wege*, Op. 87
    GB:Lbm (h.1549.)

*Farewell, Song without Words*
    GB:Lbm (h.1549.)

*Fischerlied*, Op. 43
    GB:Lbm (h.1549.)

*Im grinen Hain* (Song without words)
    GB:Lbm (h.1544.)

*In der Waldschenke* (Rustic dance), Op. 377
    GB:Lbm (h.1544.a.)

*Priere à la Madonne*
    GB:Lbm (h.1544.)

## Lehnhardt, Gustav

*Kaiser Wilhelm's Lieblings-Melodien … für Militair--Musik*
EP  (Berlin, 1886)
    GB:Lbm (h.1508.b.[6.])

## Lehnhardt, Julius

The following works were published, 1886–1887, in Berlin.

*An die Gewehere!*, Op. 18
    GB:Lbm (h.1508.b.18.])

*Mit Gott für Kaiser und Reich*, Op. 16
    GB:Lbm (h.1508.b.[7.])

*Ordre de Bataille*, Op. 20
    GB:Lbm (h.1508.b.18.])

*Der Regimentskamerad*, Op. 24
    GB:Lbm (h.1508.b.19.])

*Sanct Hubertus*, Op. 26
    GB:Lbm (h.1508.b.[9.])

*Schneidige Truppe,* Op. 17
    GB:Lbm (h.1508.b.17.])

## Leye, L.

*Quintetto*, for 1001-02, clarinet or Basset horn, and piano
EP  (Coburg, 1850)
    GB:Lbm (R.M.17.f.15. [2.])

## Liebig, ?

*Gruss an Ems, Quick March*
EP  (London, 1880)
    GB:Lbm (h.1549.)

*Aus Freundschaft, Polka*
EP   (London, 1880)
    GB:Lbm (h.1549.)

## Lindpaintner, Peter (1791–1856)

*Frühlingslied* (1830, Schiller's Death day)
MS  SATB, B solo, 2222-02
    BRD:Sl (H.B.XVII, Nr. 390)

*Psalm zur Confirmationsferir*, 1832
MS  SATB, winds [autograph]
    BRD:Sl (H.B.XVII, Nr. 881, Kaps.)

[9] *Chorales* (1830, arr. from *Christmann-Knechschien Choralbuches* v. Jahre, 1799)
MS  2222-223, timp, contra bass, perhaps SATB
    BRD:Sl (H.B.XVII, Nr. 880)

*Schlummerlied* (1841)
MS  SSTBB, 1010-06
    BRD:Sl (H.B.XVII, Nr. 867)

*Quadrille zum Königlichen Caroussel*, 1839
MS  large band
    BRD:Sl (H.B.XVII, Nr. 813)
    This collection includes an original work, plus Lindpaintner's arr. of music by Meyerbeer, Herold, Auber, Bellini, and Strauss.

*Württemberger Lied* (1842)
MS  SATB, T solo, wind orchestra
    BRD:Sl (H.B.XVII, Nr. 398) [on 'Von dir 0 Vaterland zu Singen,' by Fr. Ritter; for the poet's funeral]

*Concertante* in B♭
MS  1111-01 (with piano added later)
    BRD:Sl (H.B.XVII, Nr. 372)

*Ouverture Militaire*
MS  large band
    BRD:Sl (H.B.XVII, Nr. 371) [arr. from a ballet overture by 'Zeita']

*Die Tochter der Linst* (Theatermusik von Raupach, 1834)
MS  1202-243, timp.
    BRD:Sl (H.B.XVII, Nr. 363)

## Lortzing, Gustav (1801–1851)

*Fest-Ouverture*
EP   (London, 1894, without indication of arranger)
  GB:Lbm (h.1549.)

## Mendelssohn, Felix (1809–1847)

*Todeslied der Bojeren* (Düsseldorf, 1834)
EP   male chorus and winds (published in Volume 4, *Works of Immermann*. (Düsseldorf, Schalub) Lost [Rietz]

*Festsgesang* (1840, for the festival in honor of printing, St. Thomas Church, Leipzig)
MS   male chorus and brass band
  Lost [Rietz]

*Festgesang an die Künstler*, Op. 68 (male chorus and brass)
EP   (Bonn, 1846)
  GB:Lbm (H.1096.i.)

*Marches* (for church processions at Düsseldorf, 1833)
MS   small military band
  Lost [Rietz]

*Ouverture für Harmonienusik*, Op. 24
EP   (Bonn, 1852)
  GB:Lbm (Hirsch M.280)

## Merzdorf, A.

*Im Brautschmuck, Polonaise*
EP   (London, 1883)
  GB:Lbm (h.1544.)

## Methfessel, Albert Gottlieb (1785–1869)

*Das deutsdle Lied*, Op. 109 (male chorus and brass)
EP   (Leipzig, 1865)
  GB:Lbm (H.1654.h.[11.])

## Meyerbeer, Giacomo (1791–1864)

*Stella del Nord* 'Symphonia per fanfare'
MS
  I:Lg

*Der bayerische Schutzen-Marsch*
MS  (orig: TTBB and brass)
     I:Mc (Noseda) [Library catalog says for 'orchestra,' but that is incorrect.]

*Fackeltanz* Nr. 1
EP   band
     I:Mc (A.45.26.5)
EP   (Berlin, 1854) [arr. Wieprecht]
     GB:Lbm (h.1570. [2.] ) 

*Fackeltanz* Nr. 2
EP   band
     I:Mc (A.45.26.6)
EP   (Berlin, 1854) [arr. Wieprecht]
     GB:Lbm (h.1570.[3.])

*Fackeltanz* Nr. 3
MS   band
     I:Fc (D.XII.28) [arr. Bimboni]
     I :Mscala [autograph, piano version, 'Nice, March 1858']
EP   (Berlin, 1853) [arr. Wieprecht]
     GB:Lbm (Hirsdl M.292)
     GB:Lbm (e.65) [a reissue]

*Fackeltanz* Nr. 4
EP   band
     I:Mc (A.45.26.7)

*Marche militaire* (by P. Viardot)
EP   band (arr. by Wieprecht, 1871)
     GB:Lbm (e.370.[14.])

## Mohr, Hermann (1830–1896)

*Am Altare der Wahrheit*, Weihgesang, for Male chorus and brass
EP   (Berlin, 1882)
     GB:Lbm (H.1795.a.[16.])

*An das deutsene Vaterland*, for Male chorus and brass
EP   (?, 1888)
     GB:Lbm (E.866)

*The Facile* quick step
EP   (London, 1873), for brass band
     GB:Lbm (f.402.c.[39.])

*Parrot Polka*
EP   (London, 1877)
  GB:Lbm (f.401.i.[22.])

*Wiedersehen* march
EP   (London, 1879)
  GB:Lbm (f.401.o.[33.])

**Morelly, L.**

*Carnevals Polka*
EP   (London, 1867)
  GB:Lbm (h.1549.)

*Les Graces, Polka*
EP   (London, 1858)
  GB:Lbm (h.1544.)

*Gossmann Tanze Walzer*
EP   (London, 1859)
  GB:Lbm (h.1544.)

**Muth, August**

*Die schonen Schweizerinnen, Ländler* (with two solo trunpets)
EP   (Hannover, Oertel, 1881)
  GB:Lbm (h.1508.b.[14.]

**Oberthür, Carl (1819–1895)**

*Festival March*, 'Charlemagne'
EP   (London, 1882)
  GB:Lbm (h.1549.)

**Ochs, Siegfried (1858–1929)**

*Ein deutsdles Volkslied* ... im Style alterer und neuer Meister
EP   band (London, 1887)
  GB:Lbm (h.1549.)
MP   www.whitwellbooks.com

**Pfeiffer, Joharm**

*Der Gemütliche Polka mazurka*
EP   (London, 1865)
  GB:Lbm (h.1544.)

## Piefke, Gottfried (1817–1884)

*Loreley Polka*
EP   (London, 1885)
   GB:Lbm (h.1544.)

## Posse, ?

*Körniggratzer Strum Galop*
EP   (London, 1867)
   GB:Lbm (h.1544.)

## Raff, Joachim (1822–1882)

*Sinfonietta*, Op. 188
MS   wind ensemble
   I:Bc (score)

## Riede, ?

*Jägers Lust Galop*
EP   (London, 1880)
   GB:Lbm (h.1549.)

## Roth, Franz

*Nur schnell Galop*
EP   (London, 1865)
   GB:Lbm (h.1544.)

*Unter Kreuzband Galop*
EP   (London, 1876)
   GB:Lbm (h.1544.)

## Rudel, ?

*Soldatenmuth waltz*
EP   (London, 1877)
   GB:Lbm (f.413.e.[11.]), for brass band

## Saro, Heinrich (1827–1891)

*Der 27 Januar Marsch*
MS   band
   I:Ria (ms. 83)

*Kaiser Franz Joseph Marsch*
MS  band
   I:Ria (ms.359)

## Scherer, ?

*Parthia*
MS  solo flute with 222-02, contrabsn
   I:OS (Mss.Mus.B.2782)

*Parthia*
MS  1122-02
   I:OS (Mss.Mus.B.4736) [one horn part is found together with Mss.Mus.B.2782]

## Schnabel, Joseph Ignaz (1767–1831)

*Missa* in D minor
MS  4 voices, 22-32, org.
   I:BGc (Mayr.265.31)

## Snelling, H.J.

*The Adieu Valse*
EP  (London, 1865)
   GB:Lbm (h.1544.)

## Sobeck, Johann (1831–1940 !)

*Quintett* in F (1111,01)
EP  (Berlin, 1879)
   GB:Lbm (h.2785.a.[7.])

*Zwei Quintette*, Op. 14, in G minor
EP  (Leipzig, 1891), for 1111-01
   GB:Lbm (h.2785.n.[1.])

*Viertes quintett*, Op. 23 (1111-01)
EP  (Hannover, 1897)
   GB:Lbm (h.2784.p.[9.])

## Spohr, Ludwig (1784–1859)

*Festmarsch* componirt zur vermählungsfeier ihr Hoheiten der Prinzessin Marie von Hessen
   und des Herzogs Bernhard von Sachsen-Meiningen den 23ten März 1825
EP  (Leipzig, 1884) [instrunentation unknown]
   GB:Lbm (f.244.yy.[5.])

**Stasny, ?**

*Polka, Im Bluthenschmuck*
EP   (London, 1878)
    GB:Lbm (h.1544.)

**Thouret, Georg (1855–1924)**

*Grosser Tusch und Fanfaren* beim Vorzeigen der Schilde, aus der Musik zun Turnier … in
    Potsdam an 13 Juli 1829
EP   (Leipzig, 1897)
    GB:Lbm (h.1206.)

*Musik am preussischen Hof* … Zwei altenglische Short Troops
EP   (Leipzig, 1896)
    GB:Lbm (R.M.16 .f.9.)

**Tutsch, Georg**

*Walzer*
MS   band
    I:OS (Ms.Mus.B.4850)

**Unrath, ?**

*Konig Karl Marcia*
MS   band
    I:FEM

**Unterlegner, F. A.**

*Gebeth vor der Schlacht*
MS   TTBB, brass band
    I:Mc (Noseda)

**Vollmar, Heinrich (1839–1915)**

The following works were published, 1876–1883, in London.

*En Bataille*, quick march
    GB:Lbm (f.401.x.[10.])

*Gruss an den Haag*, quick step
    GB:Lbm (f.401.h.[7.])

*Resoluten* quick march
GB:Lbm (f.401.x.[11.])

*Royal Palace* quick step
GB:Lbm (f.401.h.[8.])

*Walkomgroet,* salute quick march
GB:Lbm (f.401.x.[12.])

## Voss, ?

*Freikugeln Quadrille*
EP   (London, 1880)
GB:Lbm (h.1549.)

## Wallerstein, Anton (1813–1892)

*La Belle de Bruges, Polka*
EP   (London, 1870)
GB:Lbm (h.1549.)

*Pour prendre congé, Polka*
EP   (London, 1871)
GB:Lbm (h.1549.)

## Weber, Bernhard Anselm (1766–1821)

*Musik zu der Schillerchen Tragödie, Die Jungfrau von Orleans*; Act 4, Buhnennusik
MS   22-02
BRD:Sl (H.B.XVII, Nr. 654, Kaps.)

## Widnann, Wilhelm

*König Karl's Regierungs Jubilumus Festmarsch,* 1889
MS   large band
BRD:Sl (H.B.XVII, Nr. 930)

# Great Britain

## Collections

6 *Marches*
EP  (London, 1870, Boose's military Journal, Ser. 28, Nr. 5)
   GB:Lbm (h.1549.)
   Contains works by Haron, Czermak, A. Labitzky, Jacobi, and Burckhardt.

6 *Marches*
EP  (London, 1871, Boose's military Journal, Ser. 31, Nr. 5)
   GB:Lbm (h.1549.)
   Contains works by Kuhner, Ludwig, and Faust.

6 *Marches*
EP  (London, 1871, Boose's military Journal, Ser. 37, Nr. 6)
   GB:Lbm (h.1549.)
   Contains works by Baryzehnikoff, Kuhner, Piefke, Reinioch, and Gerold.

6 *Marches*
EP  (London, 1871, Boose's military Journal, Ser. 48, Nr. 6)
   GB:Lbm (h.1549.)
   Contains works by Kuhner, Koenemann, Tittl, and Van Maanen.

*Six Marches*
EP  (London, 1873, Boose's military Journal, Ser. 33, Nr. 5)
   GB:Lbm (h.1549.)
   Contains works by Hamm, Heinsdorf, Kuhner and Streck.

6 *Marches*
EP  (London, 1874, Boose's military Journal, Ser. 45, Nr. 6)
   GB:Lbm (h.1549.)
   Contains works by Faust, Van Mannen, C. Godfrey, and Bonnisseau.

6 *Marches*
EP  (London, 1874, Boose's military Journal, Ser. 36, Nr. 2)
   GB:Lbm (h.1549.)
   Contains works by Hamm, Bela, Abt, Diethe, and Zumpe.

6 *Marches*
EP  (London, 1874, Boose's military Journal, Ser. 54, Nr. 5)
   GB:Lbm (h.1549.)
   Contains works by Baron, Unrath, Ludwig, Joh. Strauss, and Bilse.

6 *Marches*

EP (London, 1874, Boose's military Journal, Ser. 47, Nr. 1)
GB:Lbm (h.1549.)
Contains works by Sawerthal, Burckhardt, Gung'l, and Lubert.

*Six Marches*

EP (London, 1875, Boose's military Journal, Ser. 32, Nr. 5)
GB:Lbm (h.1549.)
Contains works by Bartolomeas, Baier, Pressel, Sawerthal and Toller.

6 *Marches*

EP (London, 1876, Boose's military Journal, Ser. 60, Nr. 6)
GB:Lbm (h.1549.)
Contains works by Kuhner, Kappey, and Koch.

6 *Marches*

EP (London, 1876, Boose's military Journal, Ser. 56, Nr. 6)
GB:Lbm (h.1549.)
Contains works by Kuhner, Kappey, Faust, and Unrath.

6 *Marches*

EP (London, 1876, Boose's military Journal, Ser. 42, Nr. 6)
GB:Lbm (h.1549.)
Contains works by Kuhner, Kistner, and Piefke.

6 *Marches*

EP (London, 1876, Boose's military Journal, Ser. 58, Nr. 5)
GB:Lbm (h.1549.)
Contains works by Kuhner, Kappey, Piefke, V. Habicht, and Brahm.

6 *Marches*

EP (London, 1877, Boose's military Journal, Ser. 35, Nr. 1)
GB:Lbm (h.1549.)
Contains marches based on 'American tunes.'

*Six Marches*

EP (London, 1878, Boose's military Journal, Ser. 26, Nr. 5)
GB:Lbm (h.1549.)
Contains works by Hamm, Kuhner, Neutzerling, Strauss, Stark, and Sydow.

10 *Marches*

EP (London, 1878, Boose's military Journal, Ser. 40, Nr. 5)
GB:Lbm (h.1549.)
The composer names are not given.

6 *Marches*

EP   (London, 1878, Boose's military Journal, Ser. 62, Nr. 6)
     GB:Lbm (h.1549.)
     Contains works by Kappey, Haine, and Unrath.

6 *Marches*

EP   (London, 1800, Boose's military Journal, Ser. 44, Nr. 3)
     GB:Lbm (h.1549.)
     Contains works by C. Hermann, J. Strauss, Budik, Piefke, A. Parlow, and
     H. Hermann)

6 *Marches*

EP   (London, 1880, Boose's military Journal, Ser. 41, Nr. 4)
     GB:Lbm (h.1549.)
     The composer names are not given.

6 *Marches*

EP   (London, 1880, Boose's military Journal, Ser. 52, Nr. 5)
     GB:Lbm (h.1549.)
     Contains works by Hamm, L. Jeschko, Suppé, Sawerthal, and Gung'l.

6 *Marches*

EP   (London, 1880, [Ser.] 38, Nr. 3)
     GB:Lbm (h.1549.)
     Contains works by Faulwetter, Sibold, Priess, and Pavlis

6 *Marches*

EP   (London, 1880, Boose's military Journal, Ser. 50, Nr. 5)
     GB:Lbm (h.1549.)
     Contains works by Pavlis, Kuhner, and Unrath.

*Six Marches*

EP   (London, 1881, Boose's military Journal, Ser. 70, Nr. 4)
     GB:Lbm (h.1549.)
     Contains works by Kempf, Faust, Oser, and Suppé.

*Six Marches*

EP   (London, 1882, Boose's military Journal, Ser. 72, Nr. 5)
     GB:Lbm (h.1549.)
     Contains works by Faust, Kuhner, Janike, Unrath, Miller, and Audran.

6 *Marches*

EP   (London, 1883, Boosey' s military Journal, Ser. 74, Nr. 5)
     GB:Lbm (h.1549.)
     Contains works by J. Strauss, Jr., Unrath, Rosenzweig, Gladman, J. P. Hansen, and W.
     A. Kilner.

*Six Marches*

EP   (London, 1889, Boosey's military Journal, Ser. 8, Nr. 4)
GB:Lbm (h.1549.)
Contains works by Kappey, Oslislo, Stanislaus, and Ackermann.

*Six Marches*

EP   (London, 1890, Boosey's military Journal, Ser. 89, Nr. 4)
GB:Lbm (h.1549.)
Contains works by Kappey, Ackermann, and C. Franklin.

*Six Marches*

EP   (London, 1893, Boosey's military Journal, Ser. 94, Nr. 4)
GB:Lbm (h.1549.)
Contains works by G. A. Cappa, Sousa, Kappey, J. Diehl, Cameron Brock and Thomas Batley.

*6 Marches*

EP   (London, Boosey's military Journal, Ser. 96, Nr. 4)
GB:Lbm (h.1549.)
Contains works by Ackermann, M. Bilton, C. Hoby.

*Six quick Marches*

EP   (London, 1884, Boosey's military Journal, Ser. 76, Nr. 5)
GB:Lbm (h.1549.)
Contains works by Vincent Pert'l, Kappey, Ackermann, and Audran

*Six quick Marches*

EP   (London, 1885, Boosey's military Journal, Ser. 78, Nr. 4)
GB:Lbm (h.1549.)
Contains works by Ellenberg, Geisse1, Reickert, Nehl, and Faust.

*Six Quick Marches*

EP   (London, 1887, Boosey's military Journal, Ser. 82, Nr. 4)
GB:Lbm (h.1549.)
Contains works by Anton Schubert, Kappey, Ackermann, Kansak, J. Arbuckle, and Kral.

*Six quick Marches*

EP   (London, 1888, Boosey's military Journal, Ser. 84, Nr. 4)
GB:Lbm (h.1549.)
Contains works by Valentine, Canthal, Paterson, Kappey, and Ackermann.

*Six quick Marches*

EP   (London, 1890, Boosey's military Journal, Ser. 88, Nr. 2)
GB:Lbm (h.1549.)
Contains works by Ackermann, Ph. Fahrbach, Jr., Kappey, and Luschwitz.

*Six quick Marches*
EP   (London, 1891, Boosey' s military Journal, Ser. 90, Nr. 5)
    GB:Lbm (h.1549.)
    Contains works by J. Diehl, A. Muth, Kappey, and Ackermann.

*Six quick Marches*
EP   (London, 1892, Boosey's military Journal, Ser. 92, Nr. 4)
    GB:Lbm (h.1549.)
    Contains works by Warwick Moore, Ackermann, W. Bentley, and H. J. Cook.

A *New Selection of Quadrilles, Waltzes and Spanish Country Dances*, performed by Mr. Gow and
    his band
EP   (Edinburgh, 1814)
    GB:Lbm (h.2605.ii.[12.])

## Anonymous

*The Guards*. Valzer
MS  band
    I:FEM

*The Marquis of Lorne quick March*
EP   (London, 1873)
    GB:Lbm (f.403.b.[47.]), for fife and drum band

*Put me in my little bed, March*
EP   (London, 1873)
    GB:Lbm (f.403.b.[46.]), for fife and drum band

*Swedish Quick March*
EP   (London, 1865)
    GB:Lbm (h.1562.)

*Alisons Quick March*
EP   (London, 1895)
    GB:Lbm (f.800.[935.])

*The Angel's call. Quick March*
EP   (London, 1895)
    GB:Lbm (f.800.[936.])

*Arcadia Quick March*
EP   (London, 1895)
    GB:Lbm (f.800.[937.1) [Cornet I only]

*Gunpowder, quick March*
EP   (London, 1876)
    GB:Lbm (f.403.c.[69.]), for fife and drum band

*Kiss me and I'll go to sleep, March*
EP   (London, 1873)
    GB:Lbm (f.403.b.[49.])

## Ackermann, ?

*Fur's Vaterland, Quick March*
EP   (London, 1893)
    GB:Lbm (h.1544.)

*When the Boys are gone, Quick March*
EP   (London, 1892)
    GB:Lbm (h.1549.).

## Adams, Stephen [pseud. For Michael Maybrick], (1841–1913)

*Mona*, a song (for solo cornet)
EP   (London, 1889)
    GB:Lbm (h.1544.)

*The Star of Bethlehem* (with solo cornet)
EP   (London, 1887)
    GB:Lbm (h.1549.)

## Asch, Georg

*Alexina, Gavotte*
EP   (London, 1894)
    GB:Lbm (h.1549.)

## Benedict, Julius (1804–1885)

*Karl und Olga Festmarsch* (AuszIüge), 1871
MS   2 military bands
    BRD:Sl (H.B.XVII, Nr. 88)

## Buchanan, John (1819–1898)

*Fair Maid of Perth Quadrille*
EP   (London, 1871)
    GB:Lbm (h.1544.])

**Clark, C.**

*Funniosities, Polka*
EP   (London, 1895)
      GB:Lbm (h.1544.)

**Conterno, G. E. (b. 1866)**

*Romanza, 'Ethel'*
EP   (London, 1895)
      GB:Lbm (h.1549.)

**Ford, Ernest (1858–1919)**

*A la russe, Mazurka*
EP   (London, 1897)
      GB:Lbm (h.1549.)

**Frayling, ?**

*Triumphal March, 'Ulundi'*
EP   (London, 1881)
      GB:Lbm (h.1544.)

**Fredhe, ?**

*The Tourist's Galop*
EP   (London, 1889)
      GB:Lbm (h.1549.)

**Fricke, C.**

*Eldorado Galop*
EP   (London, 1877)
      GB:Lbm (h.1544.)

**Haddock, George Percy (b. 1860)**

*The Soul's Awakening* (solo cornet)
EP   (London, 1893)
      GB:Lbm (h.1544.)

## Harris, Franklin (1856–1931)

*Souvenir de la russie, Fantasia on Russian folksongs*
EP   (London, 1901)
    GB:Lbm (h.1544.)

## Hartmann, Albert (1860–1952)

The following works were published in London, 1875–1892.

*Black or White*, quick step
    GB:Lbm (f.401.u.[13.])

*Choucroute, Quick Step*
    GB:Lbm (f.401.aa.[6.])

*Cold Blood*, quick march
    GB:Lbm (f.401.f.[1.])

*The Echo*, quick march
    GB:Lbm (f.401.f.[6.])

*Home, Sweet Home March*, for brass band
    GB:Lbm (f.404.[5.])

*I loved but once*, quick march
    GB:Lbm (f.401.f.[4.])

*I think of thee*, march, for brass band
    GB:Lbm (f.404.[4.])

*Let us all pull together*, quick march
    GB:Lbm (f.401.e.[12.])

*The Lord Mayor*, processional slow march
    GB:Lbm (f.401.0.[24.])

*Love Songs*, valse, for fife and drum band
    GB:Lbm (f.403.f.[28.])

*The Man of his Word, Quick March*, for brass band
    GB:Lbm (f.404.[13.])

*The Minor march*, for brass band
    GB:Lbm (f.404.[6.])

*My First Love*, quick march
    GB:Lbm (f.401.f.[7.])

*The Night Watch March*, for brass band
    GB:Lbm (f.404.[3.])

*No doubt about it,* quick march
    GB:Lbm (f.401.e.[11.])

*Oxonian* pas redoublé
    GB:Lbm (f.412.c.[4.])

*Parade March*, for brass band
    GB:Lbm (f.404.[1.])

*Pon my word* quick march
    GB:Lbm (f.401.c.[3.])

*Soldier's Love*, quick march
    GB:Lbm (f.401.f.[2.])

*Sylvester,* Galop, for fife and drum band
    GB:Lbm (f.800.[592.])

*Thy love is all the world to me*, quick march
    GB:Lbm (f.401.c.[4.])

*The Traveller March*, for brass band
    GB:Lbm (f.404.[2.])

*Weit von dir*, Valse, for fife and drum band
    GB:Lbm (f.403.f.[29.])

*When the Cannons are coming*, quick march
    GB:Lbm (f.401.f.[5.])

*Whistle polka*
    GB:Lbm (f.403.f.[30.])

*Prost* quick march
    GB:Lbm (f.401.0.[25.])
    GB:Lbm (f.401.p.[17.])

## Hartmann, Ernst (a brother to the following composer)

The following works were published in London, 1873–1885.

*Bird of the Desert, Slow March*
    GB:Lbm (f.412.p.[12.])

*The Dragoon Guards, Galop*
    GB:Lbm (f.412.p.[13.])

*Fest Slow* March, for brass band
GB:Lbm (f.402.e.[15.])

*Handicap* galop
GB:Lbm (f.401.a.[14.])

*The Hussars Waltz*
GB:Lbm (h.1549.)

*Salut de Soldat, Quick March*
GB:Lbm (f.412.p.[14.])

*Styrian* quick march
GB:Lbm (f.412.n.[5.])

## Hartmann, John, 1830-1897, Prussian

The following works were published in London, 1878–1887.

*Abide with me, Sacred Quick March* (on W. H. Monk's hymn tune)
GB:Lbm (e.372.e.[5.])

*Admiral Stosh, Quick March*
GB:Lbm (f.412.q.[4.])

*Alcibiade,* quick march
GB:Lbm (f.412.m.[20.])

*Arbucklenian Polka*
GB:Lbm (e.372.d.[8.])

*Benjamin Binns, Quick March*
GB:Lbm (e.372.e.[6.])

*Bold Robin Hood* pas redoublé
GB:Lbm (f.412.1.[10.])

*Cabulee* pas redoublé
GB:Lbm (f.412.1.[11.])

*Carte Blance Polka*
GB:Lbm (f.412.q.[2.])

*The Chanticleers, Serenade*
GB:Lbm (g.1800.[125.])

*Dosolmi, Quick March*
GB:Lbm (e.372.e.[2.])

*Dream on the Rhine, Serenade*
    GB:Lbm (f.402.e.[16.])

*Du-Du*, quick march
    GB:Lbm (f.412.m.[21.])

*English selection*
    GB:Lbm (f.412.k.[5.])

*Enola, Quick March*
    GB:Lbm (e.272.e.[1.])

*Fine and Large, Quick March*
    GB:Lbm (e.372.d.[10.])

*Frolic galop*
    GB:Lbm (f.412.1.[12.])

*Funeral March*
    GB:Lbm (f.412.e.[3.])
    GB:Lbm (f.412.1.[13.])

*Gay Luron, Quick March*
    GB:Lbm (f.402.e.[19.])

*Greta Polka*
    GB:Lbm (d.372.d.[17.])

*Hungarian Echos, Serenade*
    GB:Lbm (f.412.n.[4.])

*Irish selection*
    GB:Lbm (f.412.k.[7.])

*Jesus call us, Sunday March*
    GB:Lbm (e.372.d.[16.])

*Karousel galop*
    GB:Lbm (f.412.n.[6.])

*Maid of Athens, Troop*
    GB:Lbm (f.412.q.[1.])

*Martha* quick march
    GB:Lbm (f.412.n.[7.])

*Les Nymphs*
    GB:Lbm (f.412.q.[6.])

*Oft in Danger, Sacred Quick March*
GB:Lbm (e.372.d.[13.])

*Onward Christian Soldiers, Sacred Quick March*
GB:Lbm (e.372.d.[12.])

*Osmanli pas redoublé*
GB:Lbm (f.412.i.[15.])

*Our brave British Volunteers*, quick march
GB:Lbm (f.412.i.[14.])

*Rapid galop*
GB:Lbm (f.412.m.[17.])

*Remembrance* quick march
GB:Lbm (f.412.k.[8.])

*Ritter,* quick march
GB:Lbm (f.412.m.[22.])

*Scotch selection*
GB:Lbm (f.412.k.[6.])

*Sehnsucht nach der Heimath* (euphoniun solo with band)
GB:Lbm (f.412.p.[15.])

*Sobriquet Galop*
GB:Lbm (f.412.q.[5.])

*Sonnambula* quick march, for bugle band
GB:Lbm (f.418.[4.])

*Soudanese, Quick March*
GB:Lbm (e.372.d.[11.])

*Spirit of Love*
GB:Lbm (e.372.d.[9.])
GB:Lbn (f.414.b.[14.]), for fife and drum band

*Le Temeraire* quick march
GB:Lbm (f.412.m.[16.])

*Thorn bush* polka
GB:Lbm (f.412.m.[18.])

*Tout a la Joie,* quick march
GB:Lbm (f.413.f.[8.])

*True Blue* galop
GB:Lbm (f.412.i.[13.])

*Two Hundred Years Ago, Quick March*
GB:Lbm (e.372.e.[3.])

*Una, Polka*
GB:Lbm (e.372.e.[4.])

*Veit, Quick March*
GB:Lbm (e.372.e.[9.])

*Vita, Galop*
GB:Lbm (e.372.e.[8.])

*Young and fair, Polonaise*
GB:Lbm (f.412.q.[3.])

*The Youngest Recruit, Quick March*
GB:Lbm (f.402.e.[17.])

## Hartner, H.

The following works were published in London, 1873–1883.

*Awfully Pretty* polka, for fife and drum band
GB:Lbm (f.403.f.[31.])

*Betsy, Schottische*
GB:Lbm (f.403.f.[32.]), for fife and drum band
GB:Lbm (f.406.), for band

*Black Diamond* quick step, for brass band
GB:Lbm (f.402.c.[3.])

*Bouquet of Sparks* polka, for brass band
GB:Lbm (f.402.c.[2.])

*British Colours* troop, for fife and drum band
GB:Lbm (f.403.c.[42.])

*British Heart* quick step
GB:Lbm (f.401.r.[13.])

*Fire Away*, quick step, for brass band
GB:Lbm (f.402.c.[1.])

*Hark! the band passes*, quick march
GB:Lbm (f.401.p.[18.])

*Quicksilver* quick step, for brass band
    GB:Lbm (f.402.c.[5.])

*The Storming* galop, for brass band
    GB:Lbm (f.402.c.[4.])

*3rd Troop or Redowa*
    GB:Lbm (f.401.a.[15.])

*Trumpet and Drum polka*, for brass band
    GB:Lbm (f.402.c.[34.])

## Hawkes, Willian Henry (1830–1900)

The following works were published in London, 1877–1881.

*Agamemnon* slow march, for bugle band
    GB:Lbm (f.418.[5.])

*Agnes Sorel* quick march, for bugle band
    GB:Lbm (f.418.[6.])

*Bondebryllup* quick march on Danish melodies
    GB:Lbm (f.412.c.[6.])
    GB:Lbm (f.414.[27.J), for fife and drum band

*Burlesque* quick step
    GB:Lbm (f.412.c.[7.])

*The Cameronian* quick step
    GB:Lbm (f.412.c.[8.])

*The Camp Service Prayer*, for brass band
    GB:Lbm (f.413.b.[7.])

*Colleen Bawn* quick step
    GB:Lbm (f.412.c.[9.])

*Cremorne March* quick step
    GB:Lbm (f.412.c.[10.])

*Danish March* quick step
    GB:Lbm (f.412.c.[11.])

*Eolian* quick march, for bugle band
    GB:Lbm (f.418.[7.])

*Erin* quick march
    GB:Lbm (f.412.c.[12.])

*Euphonium* quick march
    GB:Lbm (f.412.c.[18.])

*Fandango,* Spanish march, for fife and drum band
    GB:Lbm (f.414.[28.])

*First Love* quick march, for brass band
    GB:Lbm (f.413.b.[8.])

*French Bouquet* quadrille, for brass band
    GB:Lbm (f.413.b.[9.])

*Gaily the Troubadour* quick march, for fife and drum band
    GB:Lbm (f.414.[29.])

*German Bouquet* valses
    GB:Lbm (f.412.c.[15.])

*Gisella* quick march, for brass band
    GB:Lbm (f.413.b.[11.])

*The Hunter*, quick march, for fife and drum band
    GB:Lbm (f.414.a.[33.])

*The Irresistible* quick march, for brass band
    GB:Lbm (f.413.b.[12.])

*Jemmy Smyke Polka*
    GB:Lbm (f.412.c.[16.])

*Keel row*, Quick March, for fife and drum band
    GB:Lbm (f.414.a.[30.])

*Lady Godiva* quick march, for brass band
    GB:Lbm (f.413.b.[13.])

*Leah* quick step
    GB:Lbm (f.412.c.[17.])

*The Lincolnshire Poacher Quick March*, for fife and drum band
    GB:Lbm (f.414.a.[31.])

*Little Mary's Song, Quick March*, for fife and drum band
    GB:Lbm (f.414.a.[29.]) [missing 2nd & 3rd B♭ flute parts]

*Lucia di Lanmemoor* quick march, for brass band
    GB:Lbm (f.413.b.[15.])

*Marasquino* troop, for bugle band
    GB:Lbm (f.418.[8.])

*The Men of Glamorgan* quick march, for bugle band
GB:Lbm (f.418.[9.])

*The Mormons* quick march, for brass band
GB:Lbm (f.413.b.[16.])

*Mulligan Guards*, quick march, for fife and drum band
GB:Lbm (f.414.[30.])

*Musical Times* quick step
GB:Lbm (f.412.c.[18.])

*The Nemesis* slow march, for brass band
GB:Lbm (f.413.b.[17.])

*Ninety-five, Quick March*, for fife and drum band
GB:Lbm (f.414.a.[28.]) [missing the side drum part]

*The Octoroon* quick step
GB:Lbm (f.412.c.[19.])

*Our Sailor Prince* quick march, for brass band
GB:Lbm (f.413.b.[18.])

*The Owl* quick march, for brass band
GB:Lbm (f.413.b.[19.])

*Paddle your own Canoe* quick march, for fife and drum band
GB:Lbm (f.414.[31.])

*Pal o' Mine* valse
GB:Lbm (f.412.c.[22.])

*Parade* slow march, for bugle band
GB:Lbm (f.418.[10.])

*Pepito* galop, for fife and drum band
GB:Lbm (f.414.[32.])

*Le Petit Caporal* quick step
GB:Lbm (f.412.c.[21.])

*Popular Tunes Quick March*
GB:Lbm (f.414.a.[27.]) [missing the F flute part]

*Regina* quick march, for bugle band
GB:Lbm (f.418.[11.])

*La Sonnambula* quick march, for brass band
GB:Lbm (f.413.b.[21.])

*Taglioni* polka, for fife and drum band
 GB:Lbm (f.414.[34.])

*Tommy Dodd* quick march, for fife and drum band
 GB:Lbm (f.414.[35.])

*Troop on Irish airs*, for bugle band
 GB:Lbm (f.418.[13.])

*Tropical* quick march, for bugle band
 GB:Lbm (f.418.[14.])

*Turlunette* quick march, for brass band
 GB:Lbm (f.413.b.[24.])

*Tyrolese* quick march, for bugle band
 GB:Lbm (f.418.[15.J)

## Hawks, David Shaftoe (1791–1860)

*Marches* for a military band (composer given as aged 9)
 EP   (London, l805)
 GB:Lbm (g.847.d.[12.])

*Two Marches* for clarinets, horns, bassoons and trumpet (composer given as aged 12)
 EP   (London, 1810)
 GB:Lbm (g.847.d.[13.])

## Hecker, Johann J.

The following works were published in London, 1872–1887.

*Aldershot Camp* quick march
 GB:Lbm (f.401.a.[19.])

*Always joyful*, galop
 GB:Lbm (h.1549.)

*The Bremensis march*
 GB:Lbm (f.404.[9.])

*Brighton Review* quick march
 GB:Lbm (f.401.a.[17.])

*British Cavalry* quick march
 GB:Lbm (f.401.r.[15.])

*The British Empire* quick march
 GB:Lbm (f.401.0.[14.])

*British Infantry* quick march
    GB:Lbm (f.401.r.[14.])

*The British Soldier* quick step, for brass band
    GB:Lbm (f.402.c.[7.])

*The Canadian* quick march
    GB:Lbm (f.401.0.[13.])

*Clasping Hands* valse
    GB:Lbm (f.401.k.[1.])

*The Girl I left behind me*, quick march, for fife and drum band
    GB:Lbm (f.403.f.[33.])

*Grand Selection of Welsh Airs*
    GB:Lbm (f.401.f.[8.])

*Marching Home* quick march
    GB:Lbm (f.401.a.[18.])

*On Furlough* quick march
    GB:Lbm (f.401.a.[20.])

*Prince of Wales's Volunteers* quick march, for brass band
    GB:Lbm (f.402.c.[6.])

*Queen Victoria*, Vocal galop (for band)
    GB:Lbm (h.1549.)

*The Relief March*
    GB:Lbm (f.401.aa.[7.])

*The Return Quick March*
    GB:Lbm (f.401.ee.[10.])

*Royal Fusilier's* quick march
    GB:Lbm (f.401.i.[18.])

*Die Schwebenden Geister Waltz*
    GB:Lbm (h.1544.)

*Vivat Mariane* march
    GB:Lbm (f.404.[10.])
    GB:Lbm (h.1548.) includes an arrangement by Hecker of Beethoven's *First Symphony* for band.

**Helvé, ?**

*The Colonel, Polka*
EP   (London, 1880)
    GB:Lbm (h.1544.)

**Heuval, W. [actually A.] van den**

*Prince Arthur's March*
EP   (London, 1875)
    GB:Lbm (h.1544.)

**Hewitt, C. W.**

*Himalaya Troop*
EP   (London, 1887)
    GB:Lbm (e.372.e.[12.])

*Sleeping Maggie, Quick March*
EP   (London, 1887)
    GB:Lbm (e.372.e.[11.])

*Ye Men of merry England, Quick March*
EP   (London, 1887)
    GB:Lbm (e.372.e.[10.])

**Hoby, John Charles James (1869–1938)**

*Barcarolle*
EP   (London, 1890)
    GB:Lbm (h.1549.)

*Phrynne, Intermezzo*
EP   (London, 1890)
    GB:Lbm (h.1544.)

**Hoffmann, C. L.**

*Luther Festival March*
EP   (London, 1886)
    GB:Lbm (f.412.q.[7.])

### Hofmann, Josef (1876–1957)

*Barcarolla*
EP   (London, 1889)
    GB:Lbm (h.1549.)

*Mazurka*
EP   (London, 1890)
    GB:Lbm (h.1544.)

### Hofmann, Richard (1831–1909)

*Fanfare militaire*, Op. 44
EP   (Hannover, 1886)
    GB:Lbm (h.1508.b.[2.])

*Trompeten-Schule*
EP   (Leipzig, 1879)
    GB:Lbm (h.2270.[4.])

### Hopkins, J.

*Thanksgiving, Sacred March*
EP   (London, 1880)
    GB:Lbm (h.1544.)

### Horton, Florence

*Valse, 'Annie'*
EP   (London, 1894)
    GB:Lbm (h.1549.)

### Hume, James Ord (1864–1932)

The following works were published in London, 1893–1900. This composer also had numerous compositions published during the first years of the twentieth century.

*Lucerne Mazurka*
    GB:Lbm (h.1544.)

*Eine Nacht in der Schweitz* (with solo cornet)
    GB:Lbm (h.1549.)

*Fantasia, 'A Pastoral Scene'*
    GB:Lbm (h.1549.)

*Frauen Verein Quadrille*
    GB:Lbm (kh.1544.)

*Quick Marches*, Nr. 1–12
    GB:Lbm (f.800.[600.]) [bugle and drum parts only]

*Second to none*, Quick March
    GB:Lbm (f.800.[667.]) [fife and drum band]

## Hunter, ?

*Quick Step on 'Hearts are Trumps'*
EP    (London, 1887, for fife and drum band)
    GB:Lbm (f.403.g.[25.])

## Infantry

*Infantry Bugle Calls, with words adapted and Instructions for Buglers*
EP    (London, 1900)
    GB:Lbm (a.300.f.[1.])

*Infantry Bugle Sounds*
EP    (London, 1860)
    GB:Lbm (a.297.)

*Infantry Bugle Sounds … To be used … by command of His Royal Highness General Commanding in Chief*
EP    (London, 1873)
    GB:Lbm (8824.a.20.)

*Infantry Bugle Sounds*
EP    (London, 1879)
    GB:Lbm (a.300.[1.])

*Infantry Bugle Sounds*
EP    (London, 1885)
    GB:Lbm (a.300.c.[3.])

## Inglis, Alexander Wood (1845–1929)

*Regimental Music* (with historical notes)
EP    (Dublin, 1915)
    GB:Lbm (L.R.33.b.[2.])

## Instructions

*Complete Instructions, for the Fife* ... To which is added a collection of the most favorite marches, airs etc., performed by the Guards.
EP   (London, 1808)
    GB:Lbm (c.250.h.)

*Complete Instructions for the improved patent double Flageolet*, to which are added a Collection of airs.
EP   (London, 1825)
    GB:Lbm (b.128.[2.])

*Instruction and Duty for the Bugle, Drum & Flute for use in the Royal Navy*
EP   (London, 1901)
    GB:Lbm (a.301.a.)

*Instructions for playing the Bagpipe* containing the easiest and most approved Rule for Learners, to which is added a favorite Collection of Reels, Songs, Airs, etc.
EP   (London, 1805)
    GB:Lbm (b.175.f.)

*Instructions for the deep toned Pipe.*
EP   (London, 1854)
    GB:Lbm (H.1980.[213.])

*Instructions for the new perfected Ocarina* with tuning slide.
EP   (London, 1879)
    GB:Lbm (e.212.a.[8.])

*New and complete Instructions for the German Flute* ... to which is added a favorite Collection of Marches, Song-Tunes, Duetts, etc., and a Set of Preludes. Also the method of Double Tongueing, etc.
EP   (London, 1815)
    GB:Lbm (b.170.d.)

*New Instruction for the Mezzetti's Ocarina*
EP   (London, 1890)
    GB:Lbm (f.759.ff.[3.])

*Popular instruction book for the clarionet*
EP   (London, 1858)
    GB:Lbm (e.214.[7.])

## Jefferson, William Arthur

*The National Diamond Jubilee March*
EP   (London, 1897)
    GB:Lbm (h.1544.)

## Jones, J. G.

*Jones's Military Journal*: containing the most popular overtures, marches, quadrilles, waltzes, polkas …
EP   (London, 1852)
    GB:Lbm (h.l550.)

## Jones, James Sidney (1861–1946)

The following works were published, 1872–1890, in London.

*The Bandmaster*
    GB:Lbm (e.332.)

The Brigade march
    GB:Lbm (f.401.b.[1.])

*The Brigade* quadrilles
    GB:Lbm (f.402.c.[14.]), for brass band

*The Bugler's redowa*
    GB:Lbm (f.401.b.[2.])

*The Chanpion* quick march
    GB:Lbm (f.402.c.[16.]), for brass band
    GB:Lbm (f.403.a.[20.]), for fife and drum band

*Dolly Varden* schottische, for fife and drum band
    GB:Lbm (f.403.a.[27.])

*Driven from Home*, quick step
    GB:Lbn (f.403.a.[23.]), for fife and drum band

*Grand Comic Fantasia*, Here, There and Everywhere
    GB:Lbm (f.402.c.[13.])

*Kiss me and I'll go to sleep*, quick step
    GB:Lbm (f.402.c.[l5.]), [for brass band

*Master Robin Polka*
    GB:Lbm (f.403.a.[28.]), for fife and drum band

*The Mill Wheel troop*
    GB:Lbm (f.401.b.[3.])

*Polka, 'U-pi-dee'*
    GB:Lbm (f.403.a.[29.]), for fife and drum band

*Put me in my little bed*, quick step
    GB:Lbm (f.402.c.[17.]), for brass band

*The Silver King Quick Step*
    GB:Lbm (f.401.ee.[13.])

*To the Chasing Butterflies* quick march
    GB:Lbm (f.402.c.[11.]), for brass band

*Troop 'Sweet Love arise'*
    GB:Lbm (f.403.a.[25.]), for fife and drum band
    GB:Lbm (f.401.b.[4.])

*The Wee Dog galop .*
    GB:Lbm (f.402.c.[12.]), for brass band
    GB:Lbm (f.403.a.[26.]), for fife and drum band

*Welcome Home Quick Step*
    GB:Lbm (f.401.ee.[14.])

*The Winning Hazard March*
    GB:Lbm (f.402.a.[22.]), for fife and drum band

## Jones, W. Grant

*Izetta, Polka*
EP   (London, 1894)
    GB:Lbm (h.1549.)

## Joyce, F.

The following were published, 1872–1892, in London.

*Divisional Quick March*
    GB:Lbm (f.40l.aa.[9.])

*Fathers Love, Quick march*
    GB:Lbm (f.800.[685.]), for fife and drum band

*Old Guard Polka*
    GB:Lbm (f.800.[686.]), for fife and drum band

*Paragon Quick march*
      GB:Lbm (f.800.[688.])

*Village Ball Polka*
      GB:Lbm (f.800.[690.]), for fife and drum band

*Worcestershire Quick March*
      GB:Lbm (f.800.[691.]), for fife and drum band

## Kappey, Jacob Adam (1825–1907)

The following were published, 1878–1903, in London.

*Gavotte, 'Abschied'*
      GB:Lbm (h.1549.)

*Euphonium Solo on Airs from Donizetti's 'Maria di Rohan'*
      GB:Lbm (h.1544.)

*Clarinet solo on Airs from Donizetti's 'I Martiri'*
      GB:Lbm (h.1549.)

*Cornet solo, 'The Artiste's'*
      GB:Lbm (h.1549.)

*Boosey's Church Parade Journal* ('Sunday music for church …')
      GB:Lbm (a.217.)

*Fantasia*, 'A Burlesque'
      GB:Lbm (h.1549.)

*Clematis*, Mazurka
      GB:Lbm (h.1544.)

*The Diamond Jubilee*, Grand patriotic fantasia
      GB:Lbm (h.1549.)

*Episodes in a Soldier's Life*, Grand national Fantasia
      GB:Lbm (h.1549.)

*Fantasia on National Songs of Germany*
      GB:Lbm (h.1549.)

*Fantasia on new & popular Ballads*
      GB:Lbm (h.1549.)

*Fantasia on popular Ballads*, Nr. 2
      GB:Lbm (h.1544.)

*Fantasia on popular Ballads*, Nr. 3
GB:Lbm (h.1544.)

*The Flying Squadron*, Fantasia on patriotic nautical melodies
GB:Lbm (h.1549.)

*Fantasia*, 'French Melodies'
GB:Lbm (h.1549.)

*Fantasia*, 'Hilbernian Bouquet'
GB:Lbm (h.1549.)

*Fantasia*, 'The Last Rose of Summer'
GB:Lbm (h.1549.)

*Cornet solo. Polonaise concertante*
GB:Lbm (h.1549.)

*Recollections of Wales*, Fantasia
GB:Lbm (h.1549.)

*Rule Britannia*, Grand potpourrie on English airs
GB:Lbm (h.1549.)

*Selection of Plantation Songs and American Melodies*
GB:Lbm (h.1544.)

*Terpsichoreana*, Grand potpourrie of national dances
GB:Lbm (h.1549.)

*Under the British Flag*, Fantasia
GB:Lbm (h.1544.)

*Paraphrase,* 'Ye Banks and Braes o'bonnie Doon'
GB:Lbm (h.1549.)

*'Yule-tide,' a Christmas Fantasia*
GB:Lbm (h.1549.)

Kappey also published a number of individal tutors

Althorn in E♭ & Baritone in B♭
GB:Lbm (h.1551.a.[2.])

Brass band
GB:Lbm (h.1531.)

Clarionet
GB:Lbm (H.2891. [19.])

Bombardon
GB:Lbm (h.1551.a.[3.])

Euphoniun
GB:Lbm (h.1551.a.[5.])

Tenor Trombone and Bass Trombone
GB:Lbm (h.1551.a.[6.])

## Kaps, Karl

*Arabian Nights Quadrille*
EP   (London, 1896)
GB:Lbm (h.1544)

## Klussmann, Henry

*The Royal Princes Polka*
EP   (London: Lafleur, 1887, for fife and drum band)
GB:Lbm (f.403.g.[30.])

## Koenig, Herman (1827–1898)

The following works were published in London, 1845–1877.

*The Bohemian Polka*
GB:Lbm (h.1543.)

*Eclipse Polka* (solo cornet with Octet band)
GB:Lbm (f.411.b.[5.])

*The Postillon Polka*
GB:Lbm (h.1543.)

*Rataplan*, Cornet polka with Octet band
GB:Lbm (f.411.b.[6.])

*The Staff Polka*
GB:Lbm (h.1543.)

*Valse d'amour*
GB:Lbm (h.1543.)

*Zerlina Waltz*
GB:Lbm (h.1543.)

## Kottaun, Celian

*Billy Blowhard, Concert polka*
EP   (New York, Carl Fischer, 1909)
   GB:Lbm (f.800.[723.])

The following works were published in London, 1882–1911.

*Danse de Czechs*, for fife and drum band
   GB:Lbm (f.414.a.[41.])

*Danse liliputienne*
   GB:Lbm (h.1549.)

*Jubilee Gavotte*
   GB: Lbm (f.412.q.[12.])

*Little Mother, Concert March*
   GB:Lbm (h.1549.)

*La Mantilla*, Spanish dance, for fife and drum band
   GB:Lbm (f.414.a.[43.])

*Gavotte, 'Princess May'*
   GB:Lbm (h.1549.)

*St. Cecilia March*
   GB:Lbm (f.412.q.[11.])
   GB:Lbm (f.414.a. [42.]) [for fife and drum band)

*Venus Gavotte*
   GB:Lbm (f.800.[724.])

## Laroche, Pierre

*The Great Excitement Galop*
EP   (London, 1862)
   GB:Lbm (h.1562.)

*Rosalie Valse*
EP   (London, 1862)
   GB:Lbm (h.1562.)

## Laurent, H.

The following works were published in London, 1859–1871.
*Beloved Star Valse*
   GB:Lbm (h.1549.)

*Bianca Valse*
   GB:Lbm (h.1549.)

*The Christy Minstrels Valse*
   GB:Lbm (h.1544.)

*Dinorah Valse*
   GB:Lbm (h.1544.)

*EgyptianPolka*
   GB:Lbm (h.1549.)

*Lord Lovell's Waltz*
   GB:Lbm (h.1544.)

*The Maud Valse*
   GB:Lbm (h.1549.)

*St. Patrick's Quadrille*
   GB:Lbm (h.1549.)

*Satanella Valse*
   GB:Lbm (h.1544.)

*Second Set of Lancers*
   GB:Lbm (h.1544.)

## Lee, J. S.

*En Route, Quick March*
EP   (Londobn, 1886)
   GB:Lbm (a.237.b.[4.])

*Semplice, Gavotte*
EP   (London, 1892)
   GB:Lbm (f.800.[805.])

## Lee, Walter H.

*Maraschino galop*
EP   (London, 1878)
   GB:Lbm (f.401.k.[3.])

## Levy, J.

*Emily* polka
EP   (London, 1878)
   GB:Lbm (f.401.k.[4.])

*Levy-athen* polka
EP   (London, 1877)
    GB:Lbm (f.413.b.[31.]), for brass band

*The Promenade Polka*
EP   (London, 187 8)
    GB:Lbm (f.402.f.[16.]), for brass band

## Liddell, John

*The Mayflower* (On popular American airs)
EP   (London, 1887)
    GB:Lbm (h.1544.)

*Nell Gwynne, Galop*
EP   (London, 1884)
    GB:Lbm (f.402.e.[22.]), for brass band

## Maanen, J. C. van (Dutch composer)

The following works were published 1865–1880, in London.

*Grand Fantasia on Irish Melodies*
    GB:Lbm (h.1549.)

*Grand Fantasia on old English Ditties*
    GB:Lbm (h.1549.)

*Grand Fantasia on Songs of Wales*
    GB:Lbm (h.1544.)

*Marie Wilton Valse*
    GB:Lbm (h.1544.)

*R.I.C. Galop*
    GB:Lbm (h.1544.)

## Maillard, ?

*The Hermit's Bells, Galop*
EP   (London, 1878)
    GB:Lbm (h.1544.)

**Martin, H. ('Bandmaster')**

*The New Rifle* quick step
EP   (London, 1876)
    GB:Lbm (f.403.c.[53.]), for fife and drum band
    GB:Lbm (f.401.g.[2.])

**Martin, T.**

*Magdala Galop*
EP   (London, 1869)
    GB:Lbm (h.1544.)

**Meissler, Josef [pseud., for William Marshall Hutchinson] (b. 1851)**

The following works were published, 1877–1893, in London.

*Auf der Höhe Walzer*
    GB:Lbm (f.417.[3.])

*Dream Faces, Valse*
    GB:Lbm (f.414.a.[S3.])

*Herbstlieder*, set of valses
    GB:Lbm (f.417.[4.])

*Love's golden clime*, Valses
    GB:Lbm (f.412.r.[7.])

*Me voila, Polka*
    GB:Lbm (f.412.r.[6.])

*Mein geliebtes Land Walzer*
    GB:Lbm (f.411.b.[19.])

*Morgensfruh* galop
    GB:Lbm (f.401.k.[6.])

*My little Sweetheart Valse* (with solo cornet)
    GB:Lbm (f.800.[954.])

*Valse, The Southern Breeze*
    GB:Lbm (h.1S49.)

*Thine alone, Valse*
    GB:Lbm (h.1544.)

## Millars, Francis Joseph Haydn

The following works were published, 1873–1901, in London.

*And ye shall walk in silk attire.* Song
GB:Lbm (f.401.r.[16.])

*Auld Caledonia. Scotch Quick March*
GB:Lbm (f.401.bb.[5.])

*Auld Robin Gray and Bonnie Dundee,* Scotch quick march
GB:Lbm (f.401.s.[9.])

*Balaclava* grand parade march
GB:Lbm (f.401.k.[10.])

*The Balmoral new Lancers* (on Scotch melodies)
GB:Lbm (f.401.k.[10.]), brass band

*The Bivouac Quick March*
GB:Lbm (a.237.b.[7.])

*The Brave Old Oak,* parade march
GB:Lbm (f.401.g.[6.])

*Chanson d'Amour* valse on Mohawk Minstrels melodies
GB:Lbm (f.401.s.[7.])

*Chiming Bells of long ago,* quick march
GB:Lbm (f.401.k.[12.])

*The Church Parade,* sacred quick march
GB:Lbm (f.401.w.[1.])

*Evening Echoes* quadrille
GB:Lbm (f.401.s.[8.])

*The Galloping Snob of Rotten Row.* Quick March
GB:Lbm (a.237.b.[6.]), brass band
GB:Lbm (f.401.b.[10.])

*Hungarian* quick step
GB:Lbm (f.403.c.[57.]), fife and drum band

*Hurrah! for the Bonnets o' Blue* quick march
GB:Lbm (f.401.k.[7.])

*I don't know where to find 'em.* Quick march
GB:Lbm (f.401.bb.[6.])

*Intermezzo, 'Au revoir'*
    GB:Lbm (h.1549.)

*Jeremiah blow the fire, puff, puff*, quick march
    GB:Lbm (f.401.k.[11.])

*Luxemburg* quick step
    GB:Lbm (f.402.c.[33.]), for brass band

*The Old Friend* quick step
    GB:Lbm (f.402.c.[28.]) [brass band]

*Operatic lancers*
    GB:Lbm (f.401.w.[4.])

*Pal o' Mine* quick step
    GB:Lbm (f.402.c.[35.]), for brass band

*The Pandora* quick march
    GB:Lbm (f.401.w.[3.])
    GB:Lbm (f.401.bb.[8.])

*Plevna* quick step
    GB:Lbm (f.401.k.[9.])

*The Regular Army O!* Quick March
    GB:Lbm (f.401.k.[8.])

*'La Reve a toi,'* Romance
    GB:Lbm (h.1544.)

*Le Reve d'Amour*
    GB:Lbm (e.372.g.[5.])

*The Royal Trip to India*, quick march
    GB:Lbm (f.401.g.[5.])

*3 Sacred Hymns*
    GB:Lbm (f.401.ff.[11.])

*Sadowa* slow march
    GB:Lbm (f.403 .a. [36.]), for fife and drum band

*The Shamrock*, quick step
    GB:Lbm (f.431.w.[2.])

*The Smart Recruit. Quick Step*
    GB:Lbm (f.401.bb.[9.])

*Spring Drill Quick March*
   GB:Lbm (f.403.g.[36.]), fife and drum band

*They all do it.* Quadrille on popular melodies of the day
   GB:Lbm (f.402.f.[19.]), brass band

*Thoughts of Home*, quick step
   GB:Lbm (f.401.g.[7.])

*2nd Tornado* galop
   GB:Lbm (f.402.c.[31.]), brass band

*Valorous.* Quick march (with solo cornet)
   GB:Lbm (f.800.[971.])

*Visions of the past*, quick step
   GB:Lbm (f.401.i.[21.])

*Warblings at Morn*, quick step
   GB:Lbm (f.401.g.[8.])

*Grand March, 'The Watch by the Rhine'*
   GB:Lbm (h.1562.)

*Yankee Doodle* (with solo bassoon)
GB:Lbm (h.1549.)

## Miller, George (1826–1886)

The following works were published in 1898 in London.

*Are you there Moriarty?* Singing march
   GB:Lbm (F.800.[973.]), fife and drum band

*I'm going for a Soldier in the Morning.* Singing march
   GB:Lbm (f.800.[974.]), fife and drum band

*Keep in the Middle of the Road.* Singing march
   GB:Lbm (F. 800.[97 5.]), fife and drum band

*The Old Log Cabin in the Lane.* Singing march
   GB:Lbm (f.800.[976.]), fife and drum band

## Miller, George John (1853–1928, son of the above composer)

The following were published, 1873–1906, in London.

*Blenheim* quick march
   GB:Lbm (f.401.m.[16.])

*Cavalry Ball* polka
GB:Lbm (f.401.s.[10.])

*The Empty Cradle*, quick march
GB:Lbm (f.401.r.[17.])

*Fantasia on XVII Century Music, A.D. 1664*
GB:Lbm (h.3211.a. [179.])

*1st Italian quick march*
GB:Lbm (f.403 .a. [39.]) [fife and drllIl band]

*Johnny Wimple* quick march
GB:Lbm (f.401.w.[5.])

*Minerva* slow march
GB:Lbm (f.414.[41.]), fife and drum band]

*Over the Garden Wall*, quick march
GB:Lbm (f.401.q.[18.])

*Le Petit Tambour* quick march
GB:Lbm (f.418.[16.]), for bugle band

*Singing march.* Nr. 1
GB:Lbm (f.401.r.[18.])

*Solemn March*
GB:Lbm (f.800.[977.])

*'Trafalgar,' Nautical Fantasia*
GB:Lbm (h.1544.a.)

*Voyage in a Troopship*. A Nautical Fantasia
GB:Lbm (h.1548)

## Minasi, Antonio (d. 1870, born in Italy)

*Four favorite pieces* for a military band
EP   (London, 1850)
GB:Lbm (h.997.[4.])

*Le Jeu d'espirit*, set of quadrilles
EP   (London, 1846)
GB:Lbm (h.1555.[4.])

## Mitchell, J. S.

*Sur la Mer*. Valse
EP   (London, 1886)
     GB:Lbm (f.800.[984.])

## Money, William

*The Crusaders* quick march
EP   (London, 1877)
     GB:Lbm (f.412.d.[17.])

## Montgomery, William Henry (1811–1886)

*Bel Domonio* galop
EP   (London, 1873), for brass band
     GB:Lbm (f.402.c.[40.])

## Moore, Willian

*Agenoria*. Triumphal march
EP   (London, 1889)
     GB:Lbm (h.1544.)

*Daniel*. Processional March
EP   (London, 1887)
     GB:Lbm (h.1544.)

*Polka, 'The Post Horn'*
EP   (London, 1891)
     GB:Lbm (h.1562.)

## Morelli, A.

The following works were published, 1884–1898, in London.

*Alleluia*. Sacred march (with solo cornet)
     GB:Lbm (f.800.[990.])

*Comin' thro' the Rye*. Troop
     GB:Lbm (f.401.ff.[12.])

*Hail to the Lord*. Sacred march
     GB:Lbm (f.800.[992.])

*Her golden Hair*. Medley march
     GB:Lbm (f.800.[993.]), for fife and drum band

*I love thee dearly.* Napolitane March
GB:Lbm (f.401.ff.[13.])

*It's all right now.* Quick Step
GB:Lbm (f.800. [995.J), for fife and drum band

*Jessie, the Flower o' Dumblane* March
GB:Lbm (f.800.[996.])

*Killaloe.* Burlesque. Quick March
GB:Lbm (f.800.[997.])

*Lady Tom.* Quick march
GB:Lbm (f.800.[998.]), for fife and drum band

*Napoli.* Quick step
GB:Lbm (f.401.bb.[10.])

*Now we shan't be long.* Quick march
GB:Lbm (f.800.a.[2.]), for fife and drum band

*Serenade militaire*
GB:Lbm (f.800.a.[3.])

*The 78th Farewell to Edinburgh*
GB:Lbm (f.800.a.[4.]), for fife and drum band

## Morgan, T.

*The Elfins.* Quick march
EP   (London, 1896)
GB:Lbm (f.800.a.[6.]) [incomplete]

*Stepping along.* Quick march
EP   (London, 1896)
GB:Lbm (f.800.a.[7.]) [incomplete]

## Musard, ?

*The English Quadrille*
EP   (London, 1863)
GB: Lbm (h.1544.)

## Musgrave, Frank (1833–1888)

*Chere amie*
EP   (London, 1864)
GB: Lbm (h.1544.)

*Ruy Blas Valse*
EP   (London, 1862)
      GB:Lbm (h.1544.)

## Naylor, Fdvard W. (1867–1934)

*Introduction and Polacca*
EP   (London, 1896)
      GB:Lbm (h.1544.)

## Neumann, Edmund (b. 1819)

*Feodore Polka*, Op. 79
EP   (London, 1859)
      GB:Lbm (h.1544.)

## Newton, Emest Richard

*Ailsa mine* (song, with cornet solo)
EP   (London, 1896)
      GB:Lbm (h.1544.)

## Ostlere, May

*Only once more*, Valse
EP   (London, 1886)
      GB:Lbm (h.1549.)

## Parker, Henry T. (1842–1917)

*Jerusalem.* Song
EP   (London, 1884)
      GB:Lbm (f.800.a.[74.])

*March of the Trojans*
EP   (London, 1885)
      GB:Lbm (f.800.a.[75.])

*Sunlight and Shade.* Overture
EP   (London, 1897)
      GB:Lbm ( h.1544.)

## Peile, F. O. K.

*The Belle of Cairo*
EP   (London, 1897)
   GB:Lbm (h.1544.)

## Phillips, Lovell (1816–1860)

*Marche Militaire.* Slow march
EP   (London, *1884)*
   GB:Lbm (f.401.bb.[12.])

## Pierce, ?

*Papilio Polka* (with solo piccolo)
EP   (London, 1881)
   GB:Lbm (h.1544.)

## Potter, Sanuel

*The Art of Beating the Drum, with the camp, Garrison & street Duty by Note*
EP   (London, 1817)
   GB:Lbm (b.122.[2.])

*The Art of Playing the Fife, with the camp, Garrison & Street Duty*
EP   (London, 1817)
   GB:Lbm (b.122.[1.])

*A Sett of New Slow Marches, Waltz's & Quick Steps, for Fifes & Bugle Horns*
EP   (London, 1804)
   GB:Lbm (b.60.[6.])

## Prescott (earlier Lowthian), Caroline (1843–1919)

The following works were published, 1884–1898, in London.

*Fan Dance,* Entr'acte
   GB:Lbm (f.800.[898.]), for fife and drum band

*A Maid of Kent, Valse*
   GB:Lbm (h.1549.)

*Marguerite, Valse*
   GB:Lbm (f.800.[900.])

*Myosotis, Valse*
   GB:Lbm (f.800.[901.])

*The Reign of Roses, Fantasia*
     GB:Lbm (f.412.r.[4.])

*Sweet Briar, Valse*
     GB:Lbm (h.1549.)

*Venetia Valse*
     GB:Lbm (h.1562.a)

## Relle, Moritz

*Farewell Waltzes*
EP   (London, 1867)
     GB:Lbm (h.1544.)

*Polka-mazurka, 'Emily'*
EP   (London, 1888)
     GB:Lbm (h.1549.)

*Selection of Spanish Melodies*
EP   (London, 1882)
     GB:Lbm (h.1544.)

## Reyloff, Fdmund

The following works were published, 1873–1897, in London.

*Ave Maria*
     GB:Lbm (f.401.g.[10.])

*Bouree, danse Provencale*
     GB:Lbm (f.401.w.[9.])

*The Calm,* slow movement
     GB:Lbm (f.403.c.[59.]), for fife and drum band

*Chacone. Arabian dance*
     GB:Lbm (f.401.m.[17.])
     GB:Lbm (f.401.0.[35.])

*Diane de Poitiers.* Gavotte
     GB:Lbm (f.401.ff.[15.])

*En route.* Quick step
     GB:Lbm (f.401.cc.[3.])

*Fandango*
     GB:Lbm (h.1549.)

*Gavotte* in F
   GB:Lbm (f.401.c.[10.])

*Marching out* quick step
   GB:Lbn (f.402.d.[6.])

*Quite ready.* Galop
   GB:Lbm (f.401.cc.[2.])

*Rataplan.* Quick Step
   GB:Lbm (f.401.ff.[17.])

*Rigodon*
   GB:Lbm (f.401.o.[21.])

*The Sentry* quick step
   GB:Lbm (f.402.d.[4.]), for brass band

*Slow Movement* (with solo cornet or euphonium)
   GB:Lbm (f.402.d.[7.]), for brass band

*Step out* quick march
   GB:Lbm (f.402.d.[3.]), for brass band

*The Sultan of Zanzibar* march
   GB:Lbm (f.401.9.[11.])

## Richard, H.

*Cavatina* for Euphonium or Trombone
EP   (London, 1873)
   GB:Lbm (f.402.d. [8.]), with brass band

*Lizzie redowa*
EP   (London, 1876)
   GB:Lbm (f.401.9.[12.])

## Roeder, O.

*Love's Dreamland Valse*
EP   (Londonn, 1886)
   GB:Lbm (h.1549.)

*'The Salute,' Polka March*
EP   (London, 1888)
   GB:Lbm (h.1549.)

*Lancers, 'The Sultan of Mocha'*
EP   (London, 1892)
    GB:Lbm (h.1549.)

## Rogan, John Mackenzie (1855–1931)

*The Bond of Friendship Quick March*
EP   (London, 1896)
    GB:Lbm (f.800.a.[215.])

*Rogans Quick March*
EP   (London, 1896)
    GB:Lbm (f.800.a.[216.])

## Rollison, ?

*Hot Shot Quick March*
EP   (London, 1887)
    GB:Lbm (e.372.g.[11.])

## Ronalds, Mrs. ?

*Hurry Up, Polka*
EP   (London, 1881)
    GB:Lbm (h.1544.)

## Rosati, Emile

*Albertha Valse*
EP   (London, 1876)
    GB:Lbm (h.1549.)

## Saint Jacome, L. A.

The following were published, 1873–1879, in London.

*Fée des Eaux Polka*
    GB:Lbm (f.402.d.[15.]) [for brass band]

*Manchester Contest*, 1873 (with solo flute)
    GB:Lbm (h.2915.a.[28.]), for fife and drums

*New collection of quick and slow marches for regulation Bugles*
    GB:Lbm (a.300.b.[6.])

*A New Shot.* Quick Step
    GB:Lbm (f.402.f.[21.]) [for brass band]

## Schirbel, O.

*Galop, 'Chanpagne'*
EP   (London, 1891)
    GB:Lbm (h.1549.)

## Schmidt, ?

*Military potpourri*
EP   (London, 1862)
    GB:Lbm (h.1544.)

## Schubert, A.

*Gavotte, 'The First Kiss'*
EP   (London, 1887)
    GB:Lbm (h.1549.)

## Sibold, John Henry

The following works were published, 1873–1880, in London.

*Darling Nell* quick step
    GB:Lbm (f.402.d.[17.]), for brass band
    GB:Lbm (f.403.b.[11.]), for fife and drum band]

*Fantasia, 'Gems of Ireland'*
    GB:Lbm (f.402.d.[22.]), for brass band

*Gems of Scotland* fantasia
    GB:Lbm (f.402.d.[21.]), for brass band

*Il Glorioso* quick march
    GB:Lbn (f.403.b.[1.]), for fife and drum band

*God speed the Galatea*, national song
    GB:Lbm (f.402.d.[28.]), for brass band

*The Great Vance.* quick step
    GB:Lbm (f.402.d.[16.]), for brass band

*Hyde Park* quadrille
    GB:Lbm (f.403.b.[23.]), for fife and drum band

*I will stand by my friend*, quick step
　GB:Lbm (f.402.d.[20.]), for brass band
　GB:Lbm (f.403.b.[15.]), for fife and drum band

*Irish Melody* quick step
　GB:Lbm (f.402.d.[19.]) [for brass band]

*Jolly Dogs* quick march
　GB:Lbm (f.403.b.[18.]), for fife and drum band

*Napolitaine and Thinking of Home* quick step
　GB:Lbm (f.402.d.[24.]), for brass band

*Our Prince a True British Sailor*, quick march
　GB:Lbm (f.402.d.[29.]), for brass band

*Scotch Medley* quick step
　GB:Lbm (f.403.b.[12.]), for fife and drum band

*Scotland. Scotch quick step*
　GB:Lbm (f.401.m.[19.])
　GB:Lbm (f.401.r.[23.])

*Welch quick step*
　GB:Lbm (f.402.d.[23.]), for brass band

*When Cupid first from Scotland came*, Scotch quick step
　GB:Lbm (f.402.d.[25.]) [for brass band]

## Smith, A.

*Up the Alma's Height troop*
EP　(London, 1873)
　GB:Lbm (f.401.b.[23.])

## Solomon , E.

*See me dance, Polka*
EP　(London, 1889)
　GB:Lbm (h.1549.)

## Southworth, W.

*Le Muletier, Bolero*
EP　(London, 1893)
　GB:Lbm (h.1544.)

**Stahl, H.**

*The Convent Bells*, Quick March, for fife and drum band
EP   (London, 1883)
     GB:Lbm (f.414.a.[76.])

**St. Clair, W. G.**

*'Kayah than,'* Burmese national Air
EP   (London, 1887)
     GB:Lbm (h.1549.)

**St. Leger, W. N.**

*Balaclava*, Quick step
EP   (London, 1868)
     GB:Lbm (h.1549.)

**Stebbing, E. R.**

*Full inside, Quick March*, for brass band
EP   (London, 1883)
     GB:Lbm (f.402.e.[29.])

*A Street Boy's Life, Quick March*
EP   (London, 1883)
     GB:Lbm (f.412.r.[13.])

**Tidswell, J. W.**

*Old Towler* quick march
EP   (London, 1877), for brass band
     GB:Lbm (f.413.e.[18.])

*Those Evening Bells* quick march
EP   (London, 1877), for brass band
     GB:Lbm (f.413.e.[19.])

**Tinney, F. G.**

*Fenella Valse*
EP   (London, 1880)
     GB:Lbm (h.1549.)

**Toski, ?**

*My Queen of Hearts*, polka
EP   (London, 1889)
    GB:Lbm (h.1549.)

**Tovey, Cécile**

*Graceful Dance*, 'Dulcie'
EP   (London, 1895)
    GB:Lbm (h.1549.)

**Townley, Charles (1737–1805)**

*The Standard* a thousand years old, quick march
EP   (London, 1883)
    GB:Lbm (f.401.x.[9.])
    GB:Lbm (f.403.f.[48.]), for fife and drum band

**Trumpet**

*Trumpet and Bugle Sounds for all branches of the Army, Horse Guards*, War Office. 1886.
EP   (London, 1892)
    GB:Lbm (b.135.a.)

*Trumpet and Bugle sounds for mounted services and garrison artillery*, with instructions for the training of trumpters.
EP   (London, 1870)
    GB:Lbm (b.135.)

**Ulrich, ?**

*Lied*, Duet for two cornets
EP   (London, 1879)
    GB:Lbm (h.1549.)

**Waddell, James (fl. ca. 1840s)**

*Fackeltanz*
EP   (London, 1859)
    GB:Lbm (h.1544.)

## Wagner, Albert (1799–1874)

*Biarritz Galop*
EP   (London, 1864)
   GB:Lbm (h.1544.)

## Walker, George Oastlere

*The Right o' the Line* (solo cornet)
EP   (London, 1901)
   GB:Lbm (f.800.a.[474.])

## Warneford, Harry L. (late nineteenth century)

*Marche nuptiale*
EP   (London, 1893)
   GB:Lbm (h.1549.)

## Whishaw, Frederick (1854–1934)

*Fizz!* (Polka)
EP   (London, 1895)
   GB:Lbm (b.1549)

## Wiegand, George (1834–1901)

*Royal Scarlet March*, for fife and drum band
EP   (London, 1898)
   GB:Lbm (f.800.a.[496.])

## Wieland, ?

*Die Beiden Postillone Polka*, for two solo cornets
EP   (Loondon, 1876)
   GB:Lbm (h.1544)

## Williams, Warwick

The following works were published in London, 1877–1911.

*Acantha, Dance piquant*
   GB:Lbm (f.800.a.[508.])

*Air varié* (solo euphonium)
   GB:Lbm (h.1549.)

*Day and Night Quadrille*, for fife and drum band
GB:Lbm (f.414.a.[80.])

*Fun of the Fair Quadrille*
GB:Lbm (h.1549)

*Juanita*, Overture
GB:Lbm (h.1544.)

*Marie* (Intermezzo)
GB:Lbm (h.1544)

*Mars Quick March*
GB:Lbm (f.401.c.[12.])

*Nita, Valse espagnole*
GB:Lbm (h.1544.)

*Polonaise de concert* (solo cornet)
GB:Lbm (h.1549.)

*Round-about Quadrille*
GB:Lbm (h.1544)

*Sorrow and Joy*, cavatina
GB:Lbm (h.1549)

*The Stilton Parade*, Japanese two-step
GB:Lbm (h.1544.a)

*Topsy Turvy Quadrille*
GB:Lbm (h.1549)

*The Volunteer* slow march
GB:Lbm (f.40l.k.[21.])

*Le Zingare Gavotte*
GB:Lbm (f.412.r.[20.])

## Winn, Roland M. (1820–1893)

*March, 'Camp Life'*
EP   (London, 1883)
GB:Lbm (h.1549)

## Winterbottom, William (1838–1889)

*The Kassassin Galop*, for solo clarinet
EP   (London, 1883)
   GB:Lbm (h.1562.a.)

*March, 'She's as pretty as a Picture'*
EP   (London, 1881.)
   GB:Lbm (h.1562)

## Winton, S.

The following works were published in London in 1887.

*Duck-Foot Sue March*
   GB:Lbm (f.414.b.(30])

*Four Hornpipes*
   GB:Lbm (f.414.b.[31.])

*Let the Hills resound March*
   GB:Lbm (f.414.b.[32.])

*Macbeth Quick March*
   GB:Lbm (f.414.b.[33.])

# Italy

**Anonymous'**

Nr. 9 *Adagio espr.* ('für Hr. Löfler')
MS 11-01
    I:OS (mss.mus.B.3692) [incomplete]

*Adele*. Polka
MS band
    I:CRE

*Allegro* in D
MS 1021-22
    I:Colombaro: bibl. priv. Barcello (134a)

*Allegro marziale*
MS chorus and band
    I:Tr (Ob. 165)

*Andante* in D
MS 1021-22
    I:Colombaro: bibl. priv. Barcello (134c)

*Andante* in D
MS 1021-22
    I:Colombaro: bibl. priv. Barcello (l34d)

*Andante*
MS organ and winds
    I:OS (Ms.Mus.B.5079)

*Andantino per Elevazione* in F
MS 11-02
    I:REm (Mus. Sacra.LXXXIII-13)

*L'Arrivo*. Valzer
MS band
    I:CRE

*L'Assalto*. Galop
MS band
    I:CRE

*Ballabile*
MS   band
    I:OS (Ms. Mus.B.4794)

*Ballo Montecristo*. Polca
MS   band
    I:FEM

*La Battaglia di Palestro*. Fantasia
MS   band
    I:FEM

*Canon-Galloppe*
MS   band
    I:OS (Ms.Mus.B.4805)

*Capriccio per Trombone o Corno*
MS   band
    I:Gandino(Archivio Parrocchiale)

*Cavatina per tromba*
MS   band
    I:Gandino (Archivio Parrocchiale)

*Chi mi vuole*. Mazurka
MS   band
    I:CRE

*Chiara*. Tarnatelle
MS   band
    I:CDO

*Corina*. Mazurka
MS   band
    I:FEM

*Credo* in F
MS   three voices, winds
    I:Vsmc

*Dominus a dextris* in F
MS   B solo, 1021-121, organ
    I:Colombaro, Bibl. priv. Barcella (87)

*Emma*. Mazurka
MS   5 brass
    I :MAC (Mss. 71/ 8)

*Fantasia dall'opera 'Pipele'*
MS  solo trumpet and band
    I:Agnone-Emidiana

*Fantasia un Ballo in Maschera* (Verdi)
MS  band
    I:OS (Ms.Mus.B.4410) [incomplete parts]

*Fantasia sul Don Pasquale* (Donizetti)
MS  band
    I:FEM

*Fileno Milizia Mobile*. Polca
MS  band
    I:FEM

*Finale*
MS  band
    I:OS (Ms. Mus. B.4799)

*Finis*. Galoppo
MS  5 brass
    I:MAC (Ms. 71/1)

*Fiori d'arancio*. Valzer
MS  band
    I:MAC (Ms. 71/3)

*Furlana brillante*
MS  band
    I:OS (Ms.Mus.B.4800)

*Galops*
MS  band
    I:OS (Ms.Mus.B.4804)

*Gloria* in D
MS  3 voices, winds, organ
    I:Vsmc

*Gloria* in E♭
MS  3 voices, winds, organ
    I:Vsmc [incomplete]

(2) *Gloria* in B♭
MS  3 voices, winds, organ
    I:Vsmc [incomplete]

*Gloria di vari autori* in D
MS   TTB, winds
    I:NOVg (4.F)

*Gloria e Credo* in B♭
MS   TTB, band
    I:Nf

*Gloria* in B♭
MS   TTB, large band
    I:CMGd

*Gloria* in F
MS   1110-, viola (?) [no voices]
    I:BGi (506b. E.134) [score]

*Idillio estivo*. Marcia
MS   band
    I:FEM

*Ildegona. Galop*
MS   band
    I:FEM

*Inno a Vittorio Emanuelle* (May 4, 1864)
MS   band
    I:CRE

*Inno dei Lavoratori*
MS   brass band
    I:MAC (Ms. 71/2)

*Inno universitario*
MS   band
    I:MAC (Ms.Mus. 77/3)

*Inverno. Valzer*
MS   band
    I:FEM

*Kyrie* in C
MS   TTB, 1021-121, organ
    I:Colombaro, Bibl. priv. Barcella (85)

*Kyrie e Gloria* in C
MS   3 voices, 6 winds, organ
    I:Vsmc

*Marcie e Allegri* [for church use]
MS 21-02
 I:OS (Ms.Mus.B.4739)

*Marce Funebri* (1835)
MS band
 I:COR

*Marcia* N. 10 in C
MS 21-02
 I:REm (Mus.Sacra.LXXXIII-11bis)

*Marchia* in C
MS 2001-02
 I:REm (Mus.Sacra.LXXXIII-9bis)

*Marcia* N. 8
MS 11 winds
 I:REm (Mus. Sacra. LXXXIII-10)

*Marcia Funebre*
MS band
 I:OS (Ms. Mus.B.4812)

*Marcia funebre* in A minor
MS band
 I:Ria (Ms. 561)

(3) *Notturni*
MS 2001-
 I:Rvat (Mus. 148, c.153-154)

*Ora e sempre*. Mazurka
MS band
 I:CRE

*Orasion funebre*
MS band
 I:Ria (Ms. 236)

*Ordinanze del Rgt. Guardia Svizzera*
MS 201-02
 I:Mc (Noseda) [may be incomplete]

*Partitura*
MS band
 I:Tr (Ob. 334)

*Passo doppio per musica militare* (1843)
MS  band
     I:Mc (Noseda V. 50-13)

*Pastorale* in C
MS  2000-02, organ
     I:BRc (Pasini 43d, c. 5-6)

*Pezzi musicali* per banda senza titolo di autori diversi
MS  band
     I:LU

*Pezzi vari concertati*
MS  band
     I:LU

*Pezzo concertato* (based on Ponchielli's *La Gioconda*)
MS  band
     I:OS (Ms.Mus.B.3986)

*Pezzo per quartetto di fiati*
MS  2001-, Eng. horn
     I:OS (Ms.Mus.B.4759)

*Pezzo*
MS  100-02, harp
     I:OS (Ms.Mus.B.4738)

*Polacca*
MS  band
     I:OS (Ms.Mus.B.4821)

*Polonese*
MS  band
     I:OS (Ms.Mus.B.4823)

(2) *Polonese,* (6) *Valz,* (2) *Marcia,* (2) *Adagio*
MS  -4211
     I:OS (Ms.Mus.B.4824)

*Polche per banda* di autori diversi
MS  band
     I:LU

*Polka Rosella*
MS  brass band
     I:MAC (Ms. 71/5)

*Pot-pourri da Giovanna d'Arco* (Verdi)
MS  band
    I:Pi(l) (ATVd 111)

*Pot-pourri da I Due Figario* (Speranza) [1843]
MS  band
    I:OS (Ms.Mus.B.4315)

*Pot-pourri da La Traviata* (Verdi) [1891]
MS  band
    I:Agnone-Emodiana

*Reminiscenze di Dioorah* (Meyerbeer)
MS  band
    I:FEM

*Repertorio delle marce* per trombettieri
EP  (Roma, 1895)
    GB:Lbm (a.226.e.)

*Scale per apprendere* i gruppetti del flauto
MS  flute
    I:VEc (Ms)

*Scherzo* (Galop)
MS  band
    I:CRE

*Season Marcia*
MS  4 brass, piano
    I:MAC (Ms. 71/19)

*Sempre elegante*. Mazurka
MS  band
    I:CRE

[Senza titolo] (Mazurka)
MS  band
    I:CRE

*Serenata Armonie per clarinetto*
MS  band
    I:COR

*Sogno Amoroso*, Mazurca
MS  band
    I:FEM

*Sonata* per tromboncini in F (1829)
MS   trumpets, organ
      I:BRc

*Souvenir* dell' opera Beatrice di Tenda (Bellini)
MS   band
      I:COR

*Stabat mater* in B♭
MS   TTB, 201-02, organ
      I:Vlevi (CF.B.128)

*Strimpellata*. Polka
MS   brass band
      I:MAC (Ms. 71/4)

*Tantum ergo*
MS   4 voices, 20-02 'e fiati'
      I:Chioggia-Pilippini

*Tantum ergo* in F (for 'L. Ziller')
MS   13 winds
      I:OS (Ms.Mus.B.4439)

*Tantum ergo*
MS   2042-22, bass
      I:OS (Ms.Mus.B.5061)

*Tecum principium* in C
MS   T solo, clarinet solo, 1021-12, organ
      I:Colombaro Bibl. priv. Barcella (86)

*Tema con Variazioni per clarino* e Armonia
MS
      I:OS (Ms.Mus.B.4440)

*Terzetto*
MS   -111
      I:LU

*Tocchi di guerra* (per le Banda dei Reggimenti di S.R.M. il Re della due Sicilie)
MS   band
      I:Tr (Ob. 56)

*Variazioni*
MS   2 fl, flute d'amore, Eng. horn, Basset horn
      I:OS (Ms.Mus.B.4820)
      Contains three movements, of which the second is a set of variations.

*Variazioni*
MS 21-02
    I:OS (Ms.Mus.B.4828)

*Variazioni* for flute and band
MS
    I:OS (Ms.Mus.B.4827)

*Variazioni* ('per G. Greggiati, Clarinetto Principle')
MS solo clarinet, 2012-021
    I:OS (Ms.Mus.B.4825)

*Vexilla regis* in D (hymn)
MS TTB, 1221-121
    I:Fa (193-1720)

*La Villeggiatura*, arretta Napoletana (Andante)
MS band
    I:Mc (Noseda)

(6) *Walzer*
MS band
    I:OS (Ms.Mus.B.4852)

*Walzer*
MS band
    I:MAC (Ms. Mus. 71/17)

(6) *Valzer Tedischi* (1825)
MS band
    I:OS (Ms.Mus.B.486l/1-2)

[Viennese Waltz oollection]
MS band
    I:OS (Ms.Mus.B.4850)

*Introduction, 4 Walzer e Coda*
MS band
    I:OS (Ms.Mus.B.4847)

*Introduction, 4 Walzer e Coda.*
MS band
    I:OS (Ms.Mus.B.4836)

(7) *Valz*
MS band
    I:OS (Ms.Mus.B.4841)

*Valzer Vaterloo*
MS  band
   I:OS (Ms.Mus.B.4840)
   Additional waltzes for band in this library can be found under Ms.Mus.B.2973; 2974;
   4849; 4848; 4842; 4839; 4837; 4835; 4831; and 4830]

*Valtz*
MS  band
   I:PS (B. 217-34)

## Abbati, ?

*Mazurca per banda*
MS  band
   I:FEM

## Abbiati, Dionigio

*Una vittoria*, Marcia
MS  band
   I:LU

*Rosina*, Polca
MS  band
   I:LU

Mazurca
MS  band
   I:LU

## Acerbi, Domenico (1842–1921)

*Kyrie* (1866)
MS  2 voices, winds
   I:Vsmc

## Agnola, Giacomo (1761–1845)

*Tantum ergo* in E♭
MS  TTB, 200-02, cello, organ
   I:Vnm (Fondo S. Maria Formosa)

## Agostinelli, ?

6 *Concerti*
MS  3 flutes
I:Vnm (Cod.It.IV.1715)

## Albanese, Luigi (b. 1859)

*Inno trionfale* (1892)
MS  chorus and band
I:Tr (Ms.ob.369)
I:Rasc [arr. by Vessella]

## Alcampo, Matteo

*Il Giuranento di Umberto I.* Marcia
MS  band
I:Tr (Ms.ob.214)

## Alessandro, Michele d' (1859–1918)

*In morte di S.M. Umberto I.* Elegia
EP  (Milano, sd)
I:Mc (A.45.12.20)

## Aliani, Nicola

*Dixit*
MS  TTB, 200-02, org.
I:REm (Mus. Sacra LXXI-17bis)

## Aloe, Luigi d' (b. 1829)

*Marcia e Marcia* per Fanfara a sole trombe a pistoni
MS  band
I:MAC (mss. 37/22) [autograph score]

## Andolfi, Guglielmo (1847–1928)

*Piccolo studio sull' intonazione* per banda.
EP  (Milano, 1880) [score & parts]
I:Mc (A.45.1.18)

### Androet, Cesare (1827–1889)

*La Stella di Napoli.* Serenata (1869)
MS  band
    I:Tr (ob.51)

### Anna-Vanni, Giuseppe d'

*Gran Sinfonia*
MS  band
    I:Tr (ob.358)
MP  www.whitwellbooks.com

### Annoscia, Enrico

*Ouvertura* (1889)
MS  band
    I:Tr (ob.30)

### Arezzo Della Targia, Giambattista

*Estensione*
MS  1-121, ophicleide
    I:SI (A-7-1-5)

*Haec Aecipiet*
MS  STB, winds
    I:SI (A-7-1-4)

*Qui sedes*
MS  1001-101, ophicleide, viole
    I:SI (A-7-1-17)

### Aria, Giuseppe

*Viva Umberto.* Marcia sinfonica (1897)
MS  band
    I:Tr (ob. 130)

### Ascolese, Raffele (1855–1923)

*Serenata.* Valzer
MS  band
    I:MAC (mss.mus. 9/4)

## Asioli, Bonifazio (1769–1832)

(2) *Suonata* in F
MS band
    I:COR [autograph score]

## Asioli, Raffaele (1817–1899)

*Marcia funebre*
EP (Milano, 1875)
    I:Mc (A.45.2.16)

## Avalione, Vincenzo

*Sinfonia* (1878)
MS band
    I:Tr (ob. 103)
MP www.whitwellbooks.com

## Avoni, Petronio (1790–)

*Armonia sopra diversi motivi di Cimarosa* (1826)
MS 2222-221
    I:Bc

*Due Armonie* sopra … Paer e Paisielo
MS
    I:Bc

## Avseri de Chistofano, Giuseppe

*Marcia funebre* (1890)
MS band
    I:Tr (obv. 01)

## Baccherini, Francesco (fl. ca. 1815)

*Armonia*
MS Flute concerto, Piccola banda
    I:OS (mss.Musiche.B.3076)
MP www.whitwellbooks.com

*Capriccio*
MS band
    I:OS (mss.Musiche.B.1864)

### Bado, Giuseppe

*Potpourri* [Andante, Theme & Var, Moderato)
MS   1120-21
    I:Gl (sc. 154)

### Baioni, Massimo

*Canto dei militari*, Inno a S. M. Umberto I
EP   (Milano, 1893)
    I:Mc (A.45.3.2)

### Banchi, Giuseppe

*Il Risorgimento italiano*. Gran Suonata Militare
MS   Orchestra & 3 bands
    I:Tr (ob. 226)

### Baragatti, Romeo

*Grande Fantasia Musicale*
MS   band
    I:Tr (ob. 162) [for the unveiling of a monument to Vittorio Emanuale in Florence]

### Barberis, Pier Luigi

*Ad Amilcare Ponchielli compianto*, Marcia funebre
EP   (Milano, 1889)
    I:Mc (A.45.3.12)

### Bartolucci, Mariano

*Overture*
EP   (Perugia: Belati, sd)
    I:Mc (Banda.l.18)

### Baschieri, Giovanni

*ltalia e Montenegro*. Marcia Trionfale
EP   (Firenze, Lapini, 1897), band
    I:BGi (Faldone 6, n. 59) [Anesa]

**Battaglia, Giacinto (1803–1861)**

*Sinfonia*
MS  2032-221
    I:OS (Mss.Mus.B.1863)

**Bavagnoli, Manlio**

*Sinfonia Pastorale* (1888)
MS  band
    I:Fc (D.XI.2803)
MP  www.whitwellbooks.com

**(Beethoven, representative nineteenth century Italian transcriptions)**

'Adagio,' *Symphony Nr. 4*
EP  (Roma, sd)
    I:Mc (A.45.5.25)

'Adagio,' *Sonata Patetica*
EP  (Milano, 1892)
    I:Mc (A.45.5.23)

'Adagio,' *Sonata Patetica*
EP  (Rome, sd)
    I:Mc (A.45.5.24)

'Andante,' *Symphony Nr. 1*
EP  (Rome, sd)
    I:Mc (A.45.5.27)

'Andante,' *Symphony Nr. 5*
EP  (Milano, sd)
    I:Mc (A.45.5 .22)

'Andante,' *Symphony Nr. 5*
EP  (Roma, sd)
    I:Mc (A.45.5.28)

*Coriolano Overture*
EP  (Milano, 1898)
    I:Mc (A.45.5.32)

Egmont Overture
EP  (Milano, 1899)
    I:Mc (A.45.5.33)

*Fidelio Overture*
EP   (Milano, 1904)
    I:Mc (A.45.5.34)

*Grand Septuor*
MS
    I:Nc (111.1.19/4) [mss. score, arr. Michele Carada de Colobrano]

'Marcia funebre,' *Symphony Nr. 3,*
EP   (Milano, 1902)
    I:Mc (A.45.5.35)

[First movement], *Symphony Nr. 9*
EP   (Milano, 1914)
    I:Mc (A.45.5.40)

## Belli Sandre, M.

*Genitori*
MS  3 voices, winds, organ
    I:Vsmc

*Inno: O Decus coeli* in C (1869)
MS  3 voices, winds, organ
    I:Vsmc

*Tantum ergo* in B♭
MS  T, winds, organ
    I:Vsmc

## Belloli, Agostino (1778–1838)

*Ballabile*. Clerico
MS  band
    I:OS (Mss.Mus.B.4795)

Concerto per Corno e Fagotto
MS  horn, bsn, band
    I:OS (Mss.Mus.B.1535)

*Divertimento* for horn
MS  horn, band
    I:OS (Mss.Mus.B.1536)
MP  www.whitwellbooks.com

*Quintet*
MS  21-02
  I:Mc (Da Camera Ms. 2.6)

*Quintet*
MS
  I:OS (Mss.Mus.B.1538)

## Belotti, Giuseppe

*Confitebor* in C
MS  T solo, STB, 1020-222, basso, timpani, oficleide, organ
  I:Vertova(Raccolta privata Belotti) [Anesa]

*Credo* in F
MS  TTBB, solo fl, 21121, timpani, bass, organ.
  I:Vertova(Raccolta privata Belotti) [Anesa]

*Credo* in D (1863)
MS  SATTB, 1020-221, bass, organ, timpani
  I:Vertova(Raccolta privata Belotti) [Anesa]

*Credo* in E♭
MS  TTBB, 20-22, piccolo, organ
  I:Vertova(Raccolta privata Belotti) [Anesa]

*Credo* in E♭
MS  TTB, 20-221, piccolo, bass
  I:Vertova(Raccolta privata Belotti) [Anesa]

*Cum Sancto* in B♭
MS  STTBB, 1020-222, oficleide, bass, timpani, organ, piccolo
  I:Vertova(Raccolta privata Belotti) [Anesa]

*Dixit* in E♭
MS  TTB, 1020-222, bass, org, timpani
  I:Vertova(Raccolta privata Belotti) [Anesa]

*Dixit* in E♭
MS  TTBB, solo flute, solo trombone, 1020-221, timpani, bass, organ
  I:Vertova(Raccolta privata Belotti) [Anesa]

*Dixit* in F
MS  ATTB, solo flute, clarinet, and trombone, 10-221, bass, timpani, organ
  I:Vertova(Raccolta privata Belotti) [Anesa]

*Dixit* in F
MS  STB solo, TB, 1020-221, bombard, bass, timpani, organ, piccolo
    I:Vertova(Raccolta privata Belotti) [Anesa]

*Gloria* in E♭
MS  TTB, 20-121, piccolo, bass
    I:Vertova(Raccolta privata Belotti) [Anesa]

*Gloria in excelsis Deo* in E♭
MS  B solo, STT, 20-221, oficleide, bass, timpani, organ, piccolo
    I:Vertova(Raccolta privata Belotti) [Anesa]

*Inno per processione* in E♭ (*Ave Maris Stella*) [1866]
MS  STTB, 1022-223, oficleide , bass, piccolo, timpani
    I:Vertova(Raccolta privata Belotti) [Anesa]

*Iste confessor* in C
MS  TTB, 20-201, piccolo, timpani
    I:Vertova(Raccolta privata Belotti) [Anesa]

*Kyrie* in C
MS  TTB, 1020-122, bass, organ
    I:Vertova(Raccolta privata Belotti) [Anesa]

*Kyrie* in B♭
MS  TTBB, solo trumpet, trombone, 1020-11, timp, bass, organ, picc
    I:Vertova(Raccolta privata Belotti) [Anesa]

*Kyrie* in B♭
MS  TTB solo, TB, solo fl, bsn, trombone, 20-21, bass, timpani, organ
    I:Vertova(Raccolta privata Belotti) [Anesa]

*Laudamus* in G
MS  ST solo, TTB, solo flute, 20-222, oficleide, bass, timpani, organ
    I:Vertova(Raccolta privata Belotti) [Anesa]

*Litanie*
MS  STTB, 10-101, piccolo, bass, organ
    I:Vertova(Raccolta privata Belotti) [Anesa]

*Magnificat* in B♭
MS  STTB, 1020-222, bass, organ
    I:Vertova(Raccolta privata Belotti) [Anesa]

*Magnificat* in F
MS  TTB solo, TB, solo flute, clar, tpt, trombone, 10-021, bass, timpani, organ
    I:Vertova(Raccolta privata Belotti) [Anesa]

*Miserere* in A minor
MS  TTB, 1020-121, organ
      I:Vertova(Raccolta privata Belotti) [Anesa]

*Qui tollis*
MS  T, TB, solo tpt, clar, 101-121, organ
      I:Vertova(Raccolta privata Belotti) [Anesa]

*Sanctus* in C
MS  TB solo, T, solo flute, trombone, 20-221, bass, timpani, organ
      I:Vertova(Raccolta privata Belotti) [Anesa]

*Sonata con variazioni* per fagotto
MS  solo bsn, 1020-12, bass, organ
      I:Vertova(Raccolta privata Belotti) [Anesa]

*Tantum ergo* in F
MS  TB solo, TB, solo fl, bsn, 20-221, bass, timp, organ
      I:Vertova(Raccolta privata Belotti) [Anesa]

*Versetto* in C
MS  TB solo, TB, solo flute, tpt, trombone, 20-121, oficleide, timpani, organ
      I:Vertova(Raccolta privata Belotti) [Anesa]

*Versetto* in E♭
MS  TB solo, solo tpt, 20-12, bass, timpani, picc, organ
      I:Vertova(Raccolta privata Belotti) [Anesa]

*Versetto* in E♭
MS  B solo, STTB, solo tpt, trombone 1020-122, picc, bass, timp, organ, oficleide
      I:Vertova(Raccolta privata Belotti) [Anesa]

*Versetto* in E♭
MS  B, solo trombone, -001, organ, timpani
      I:Vertova(Raccolta privata Belotti) [Anesa]

*Versetto* in F
MS  S, solo horn, tpt, 1020-111, bass, organ
      I:Vertova(Raccolta privata Belotti) [Anesa]

*Versetto* in B♭
MS  T, solo tpt, fl, cl, trombone, 20-222, bass, timpani, organ
      I:Vertova(Raccolta privata Belotti) [Anesa]

*Versetto* in D♭
MS  T, STB, 1021-221, timpani, organ
      I:Vertova(Raccolta privata Belotti) [Anesa]

*Vespro* in C
MS   STB, 20-021, piccolo, bass
    I:Vertova(Raccolta privata Belotti) [Anesa]

## Beretta, Giovanni

*Lauda*
MS   4 voices, -2211
    I:Adria:Arch. del duomo

## Bernardi, Enrico (1838–1900)

*Inno Garibaldi*
EP   (Milano, 1861)
    I:Mc (A.45.6.12)

## Bertani, Natale

*Laudate Dominium*
MS   TTB, 17 winds
    I:REm (Mus.Sacra.LVIII-I0)

Laudate pueri
MS   TTB, 11 winds
    I:REm (Mus.Sacra.LVIII-14)

*Tantum ergo*
MS   TTB, 18 winds
    I:REm (Mus.Sacra.LIX-53)

## Bertini, Ernesto

(5?) *Marches*
MS   band
    I:MAC

*Laudamus*
MS   T, chorus, band
    I:MAC (Mss.Mus.18/16) [autograph]

*Oratorio*
MS   Baritone solo, chorus, band
    I:MAC (Mss. Mus.18/43)

## Bertini, Severo

*Marcia funebre* (for Vittorio Emanuale II) (1879)
MS  band
  I:Tr (ob.383)

## Bertolazzi, ?

*Preludio sinfonico* per banda
MS  band
  I:FEM

## Bianchedi, Pretro

*Due inni funebri* 'Sulla tomba di Sileno Amori' (1876)
MS  band
  I:MAC (Mss.Mus.20/6) [autograph]

## Bianchi, Giovanni

*Tantum ergo* (1836)
MS  4 voice chorus, band
  I:Fc (E.1030, S. Gaetano)

## Billi, Vincenzo (1869–1938)

*Tenebre e luce*
EP  (Firenze, Lapini), band, with solo tpt, and trombone
  I:BGi (Faldone 12, n. 104.56) [Anesa]

## Bittoni, Bernardo (1757–1829)

*Timete Domenum Omnes* (Graduale e Offertorio)
MS  STB, 111-02, st. bass
  I:MAC (A.8.5)

## Boara, Giovanni (fl. ca. 1830–1860)

*Inno del Preziosissimo Sangue* in F (1851)
MS  3 voices, winds, org.
  I:Vsmc

*Inno di S. Spiridione* in F (186 0)
MS  3 voices, winds, org.
  I:Vsmc

*Kyrie, Gloria, Credo* in B♭
MS   2 voices, winds
　　I:Vsmc

## Bonferoni, Pietro

*Pensiero sinfonicoa per Banda* (Napoli, 1878)
MS   band
　　I:Tr (ob. 231)

*Il Re all'inondazione di Verona*. Coro Sinfonico
MS   band
　　I:Tr (ob.267)

## Bongiorno, Francesco

*Inno* (1907)
MS   TTB, band
　　I:Messina-Univ.

## Bonicioli, Riccardo (1853–1933)

*Sestetto*
MS   1122-
　　I:Mc (Da Camera Ms. 3.17)

## Bonicoli, Venceslao

*Sulle rive di Killarney*. Fantasia (on Finland melodies)
MS   band
　　I:Tr (ob. 174)

## Borea, Vincenzo

*Marcia sinfonica e Preludio sinfonico*
MS   band
　　I:Tr (ob. 142)

## Braga, Giuseppe (1829–1907)

*Marcia trionfale*
MS   band
　　I:Tr (ob. 230)

## Bregoli, ?

*Duetto originale* per banda
MS
    I:FEM

## Briccialdi, Giulio (1818–1881)

*Quintetto* in B♭
MS  1111-01
    I:TE (busta 34)

## Bufalari, Carlo (late nineteenth century)

*Ballabili caratteristici e descrittivi*
MS  band
    I:Tr (ob. 44)

## Buzzolla, Antonio (1815–1871)

*Ballabile*
MS  band
    I:Adria-Conservatorio (258)

*Marcina* in F
MS  organ and winds
    I:Vsmc

## Caccavaio, Luigi

*L' Esercito italiano*. Marcia con segnali
MS  band
    I:Tr (ob.51)

*Un Pensiero a Napoli* (Fantasia)
MS  band
    I:Tr (ob. 181/1)

## Cagnola, Emilio

*Armonia* in B♭
MS  -004
    I:Fc (D.xi.2894)

## Cajani, Giuseppe

*Elegia* (9 Jan. 1884)
MS  band
  I:Tr (ob.359)

## Calamara, Gregorio

*Tantum ergo* (1882)
MS  4 voices, band
  I:Messina-Univ.

## Calecari, G. F.

[bound collection]
MS  trumpet band
  I:Mc (Noseda D.S)
  This is a collection of some 50 original compositions and arrangements for 8 trumpet
  parts, with horns and trombones, made for the Conte di Gallenberg. The collection
  begins with exercises where the arranger learned to write for the trumpets, each part
  in a different key.

## Cali, Girolano

*Savoia!* (Sinfonia, 1881.)
MS  band
  I:Tr (ob. 183)

## Califfi, ?

*Sanctus e Agnus Dei* in B♭
MS  3 voices, 9 winds
  I:Vsmc

## Calvi, ?

*Tantum ergo* in D
MS  band
  I:OS (mss.B.5058)

## Calvi, Girolano (d. 1848)

*Beatus vir*
MS  TTB, 20-101
  I:BGc (Faldone 5, n. 107) [Anesa]

*Bene benissimo* (1842)
MS  TTB, winds
    I:BGc (5.101)

*Brindisi pel Sig. Carlo Arioli* (1841)
MS  TTB, 1000-321
    I:BGc (Faldone 5, n. 104) [Anesa]

*3 Divertimenti*
MS  1021-021, piccolo, perc.
    I:BGc (Faldone 11, n. 178) [Anesa]

*Due divertimenti* in E♭
MS  1001-221, piccolo
    I:BGc (Falcbne 2, n. 40) [Anesa]

*Divertimento*
MS  2001-
    I:BGc (Faldone 2, n. 45) [Anesa]

*Finale* in E♭
MS  1002-521, piccolo
    I:BGc (Faldone 2, n. 42) [Anesa]

*Godiam godiam la vita*
MS  SSTTBB, 1022-222, 2 piccolo
    I:BGc (Faldone 5, n. 97) [Anesa]

*Inno per processione* (Mysteriun ecclesiae)
MS  TTB, 1020-001
    I:BGc (Faldone 2, n. 36) [Anesa]

*Intermezzo* (from La Corte d'Amore)
MS  2221-121, timp.
    I:BGc (15.210)

*Introduzione e pastorale* in Eb
MS  1032-121, picc
    I:BGc (Faldone 2, n. 44) [Anesa]

*Introduzione, Tema, Variazioni e Finale* per Armonia
MS  band
    I:OS (Mss.B.3156)

*Marcia* per banda in F
MS  1022-321, picc, perc
    I:BGc (Faldone 2, n. 43) [Anesa]

*Ottetto* in E♭
MS  2022-02
    I:BGc (2.38)

*Sanctorun meritis*
MS  TTB, 1000-221
    I:BGc (Faldone 4, n. 65) [Anesa]

*Serenade* in G
MS  large band
    I:BGc (Faldone 7, n. 140) [Anesa]

*Settimino* in D
MS  1021-02, cimbalo
    I:BGc (6.124)

*Settimino* in D
MS  band
    I:BGc (2.41)

*Settimino*
MS  2021-02
    I:OS (Mss.B.3155)

*Sinfonia* in D
MS  2022-221
    I:BGc (Faldone 2, n. 39) [Anesa]

*Si queris miracula.* Inno per processione
MS  TTBB, solo piccolo, 21-021
    I:BGc (Faldone 4, n. 67) [Anesa]

Vexilla
MS  TTBB, 2221-221
    I:BGc (Faldone 3, n. 51) [Anesa]

## Canti, Antonio

*Sensitiva Nr. 2* senza titolo
MS  band
    I:CRE (ms.31)

## Caporali, Luigi

*Giorno di festa.* Marcia per Banda (Padova, 1894)
EP  band
    I:BGc (Faldone D, 7, 2 (14) .37) [Anesa]

## Cappelli, Oreste

*Il Paese Italiano.* Brillante marcia mil. (1890)
MS  band
    I:Tr (ob. 306)

## Carducci, Aristodemo

*Alla Santa* (funeral march for V. Emanuale, 1878)
MS  band
    I:Tr (ob. 18)

## Carini, Cesare (b. 1841)

*Divertimento* for Clarino & banda
MS  tpt & band
    I:FEM

## Carulli, Benedetto (1797–1877)

*Quintetto*
MS  1021-01
    I:Mc (Noseda)

## Casamorata, Luigi (1807–1881)

*Armonia* di media difficolta
MS  band
    I:Fc (D.XI .194)

*Raccolta di Armonie*
MS  1122-02
    I:Fc (D.X.214-230)
    This work is based on 'classical composers for use by students of the Royal
    Institute Musicale di Firenze.']

## Cavallini, Ernesto (1807–1874)

*Fantasia*
MS  clarino & band
    I:FEM

## Cerquetelli, Giusepp (1848–1931)

*Overture* in B♭
EP   (Firenze, 1898)
      I:Mc (A.45.16.33)

## Cesari, Pietro

*A Camonens*, Marcia funebre
EP   (Milano, 1899)
      I:Mc (A.45.11.13)

*Marcia funebre* (in memory of the 1st King of Italy)
EP   (Milano, score)
      I:Mc (A.45.11.12)

## Cimino, Gabride

*Sinfonia*
MS   band
      I:Tr (ob. 146)

## Ciotti, Francesoo

*La Desolata*. Elegi-preghiera (early twentieth century)
MS   STB, band
      I:Ad (Mss.C.V/1)

## Cocoon, Nicolo (1826–1903)

*Dixit* in C
MS   2 voices, winds, organ
      I:Vsmc

*Domine ad adjuvandum* in G
MS   2 voices, winds, organ
      I:Vsmc

*Laudamus* in F
MS   TT, winds, organ
      I:Vsmc

*Libra me* (1873)
MS   TB solo, TB chorus, 20-221 , timp, organ
      I:MAC (Mss.Mus. 32/2)

*Marcia* (1874)
MS  20-222, timp, pf, st.bass
    I:PESe (Rari 1-5/I.35/a-l)

*Pastorale* in G
MS  organ, clarini, corni
    I:Vsmc

*Quoniam*
MS  B, winds, organ
    I:Vsmc

## Cocconi, ?

*Credo*
MS  BB, TB chorus, clarinets, horns
    I:Milano-S. Antonio da Padova

*Gloria*
MS  BB, TB chorus, clarinets, horns
    I:Milano-S. Antonio da Padova

*Laetatum sum* in G
MS  TB, clarinets, horns, organ
    I:NOd

*Lauda Jerusalem* in C
MS  TTBB, clarini, corni, organ
    I:VIGsa.

## Coccurullo, Felice

*La sveglia al campo.* Fantasia militare
MS  band
    I:Tr (ob. 325)

## Costa, Antonio

*Quintet* in A
MS  1011-02
    I:Gl (Sc.35)

## Cozzi, Gaetano

*Domine — Qui tollis* (1840)
MS  'a Banda'
    I:URBcap [autograph score]

*Suonata* in A♭ (1859)
MS  band
    I:URBcap

*Vergin Madre*. Preghiera
MS  Contralto and band
    I:URBcap

## Crisanti, Vincenzo (b. 1813, employed by Pio X)

*Composizione musicale per Concerto*
MS  presumed to be for band
    I:Rvat (Mus.92)

*Fanfara pontificia*
MS  presuned to be for band
    I:Rvat (Mus.103)

*Pensiero religioso* per banda
MS  band
    I:Rvat (Mus.97)

## Crotti, Giovanni

*Quintet*
MS  -041
    I:OS (mss.mus.B.1125)

## Curci, Giuseppe

*Marcia funebre* (1869)
MS  band
    I:BAR (F.GJ.A.297)

## Dacci, Giusto (1840–1905)

*Inno epitalamico*
MS  band
    I:FEM

## Daddi, Giuseppe

*Marcia funebre*
EP  (Milano, 1900)
    I:Mc (A.45.12.16)

*Marcia da processione*
EP   (Milano, 1900)
      I:Mc (A.45.12.17)

## Dall'argine, Luigi

*Magnificant* (1857)
MS   TTBB, 40-221
      I:CMGd (133)

*Tantum ergo*
MS   3 voices, 1100-121, cello, st. bass, organ
      I:PAas (n.134)

## Danese, Domenico

*Elegia funebre ... Pensiero descrittivo*
MS   large band
      I:Tr (ms.pf.101/2)

## Daniero, Francisco

*Marcia funebre* (1878, for Vittorio Emanuale)
MS   band
      I:Tr (ob.12)

## David, Adolfo

*Ronda dei Pifferari*
EP   (Milano, sd)
      I:Mc (A.45.12.25)
      The cover says 'Instr. Pio Nelli' but the work, an *Allegretto*, looks like original wind
      music. Some appears very common, but some is very lyrical. One movement, ends *pp*.

## Davide da Bergamo [Felice Moretti] (1791–1863)

[no title]
MS   band
      I:BGc (Faldone D, 7, 5 (36) .38) [Anesa]

### De Giorgi, Andrea (1836–1900)

The following manuscripts are all found in I:Gandino (Archivio Parrocchiale) as reported by Anesa.

*Armonia* in B♭
MS   10-111

*Armonia* in B♭
MS   -1, flicorno, bombardino, bombardone

*Armonia* in B♭
MS   -1, flicorno, bombardino, 2 bassi

*Armonia religiosa* in A♭
MS   30-242, clavicorno, bombardone, pelittone

*Armonia religiosa* in E♭
MS   10-111, bombardone

*Armonia religiosa* per il SS Sacramento in A♭
MS   -12, bombardino basso

*Ave Maris Stella*, in D♭
MS   TTBB, 1222-222, bombardoni, timpani, bass

(Piccola) *Ave Maris Stella* in D♭
MS   TTBB, 1020-222, bombardoni, perc.

(Breve) *Ave Maris Stella* in A♭
MS   TTB, 1222-223, bombardoni, timp

(Salmo) *Confitebor tibi Domine* in C (1880)
MS   T, chorus, 1010-121, piccolo, timpani, basso

*Credo* in B♭ (1886)
MS   TTB, 1022-123, timpani, organ

*Domine ad adjuvandum* in C
MS   TTB, 1020-122, timpani, organ, basso

*Domine ad adjuvandum* in C
MS   TTB, 1020-122, bass, timpani

*Domine ad adjuvandum* in C
MS   SSAATTBB, 1022-122, organ, bass

*Duetto* in A♭
MS   TB, chorus, 1112-222, timpani, bass, organ, piccolo

*Inno (Pange lingua)* in E♭, per processione
MS  SATB, 1020-222, timpani,

*Inno* in A♭
MS  TTBB, 1020-32 (trombe cantabili e d'accompagnamento), bombardini cantabili, bombardini, bombardoni, bassi

*Inno (Pange lingua)* in E♭, per processione
MS  TTB, 2222-222, timpani, basso

*Inno lugubre* in C minor per processione
MS  TTB, 1122-222, timpani, organ

*Inno per processione* in A♭
MS  TTB, 1030-32, bombardini, bombardoni, bassi

*Inno per processione* in B♭
MS  TTB, 1122-222, timpani

*Inno per processione (Pange lingua)* in B♭
MS  TTB, 2222-222, timpani, bass

*Inno per vespro* in C
MS  TTBB, 1020-122, timpani, bass

*(Inno) Iste confessor per processione* in D♭
MS  TTBB, 1222-223, bombardoni, tmpani, bass

*(Solenne) Iste confessor per processione* in E♭
MS  TTB, 1040-202, bombardoni, bassi, perc, piccolo, orgn

*Kyrie* in D minor
MS  TTB, 1122-122, piccolo, timpani, organ

*Kyrie* in B♭
MS  TTB, 1222-123, organ

*Laudamus, Gratias e Domine Deus* in D♭
MS  TB solo, 1022-123, timpani, organ

*Laudamus, Gratias e Domine Deus* in B♭
MS  B solo, TTB chorus, 1220-223, piccolo, organ

(Salno) *Laudate Dominun* in E
MS  B solo, chorus, 1020-123, timpani

*Litanie della B.V.*
MS  TTBB, 1020-021

(Numero quattro) *Litanie della B.V.M.*
MS   TTB, 2222-122, timpani

(Solenne) *Pange lingua*
MS   TTBB, 1220-223, bombardini, bombardoni, piccolo, perc

(Piccolo) *Pange lingua* in E♭ per processione
MS   TTBB, 1222-222, bombardoni, perc, piccolo

*Pange lingua* in B♭
MS   TTB, 1020-121, timpani, organ

*Pange lingua* in B♭
MS   SSTTB, 1030-223, timpani

(Solenne) *Pange lingua* per processione
MS   TTBB, 1222-122, piccolo

*Pezzo concertato originale*
MS   solo cl, 1030-523, flicorni, clivcorno, bombardino, timpani

*Qui sedes* in A♭
MS   B solo, trombone solo, 1021-123, timpani, organ, piccolo

(Piccolo) *Qui tollis* in G minor
MS   TTB, 1022-123, organ

*Quonian* in C
MS   T solo, TTB, 1222-123, piccolo, organ

*Salve Regina* in E♭
MS   TTB, 1020-123, timpani, organ

*Sanctus, Benedictus, e Agnus Dei* in C
MS   TTB, 1020-123, timpani, organ

*Sequenza dalla B.V. Addolorata in* F
MS   1020-123, bass, organ

*Tantum ergo* in E♭
MS   B solo, chorus, 2222-223, timpani, organ

*Tantum ergo* in D
MS   B solo, chorus, solo trumpet, trombone

*Tantum ergo* in A♭
MS   TB, tpt, trombone, organ

*Tantum ergo* in E♭
MS   TB, tpt, trombone, organ

*Tantum ergo* in E♭
MS  T solo, 1222-223, timpani, organ

*Tantum ergo* in F (1893)
MS  ST, 1022-123, timpani, organ

*Versetto* in D
MS  B solo, chorus, 1020-123, timpani, organ

*Versetto (Introduzione, Intermezzi di variazione e Finale)*
MS  TB, solo flute, horn, 1122-123, timpani, organ

*Versetto (O Salutaris hostia)* in A♭
MS  T solo, chorus, 2222-123, timpani, organ

*Versetto (Tantum ergo)* in B♭
MS  S solo, chorus, 2122-123, timpani, organ

*Versetto (Tantum ergo)* in D♭
MS  T solo, TTB chorus, 2022-123, timpani, organ

*Lungo inno per processione* in E♭
MS  SATB, 2020-221, timpani


## De Giovanni, Domenico

*Sui nostri monti.* Serenata campestre
EP  (Firenze, Lapini), 1898, for band
    I:BGi (Faldone 41, n. 436) [Anesa]


## Delle Cese, Davide (1856–1938)

*Inglesina.* Scherzo Marciabile
EP  (Firenz, Lapini), 1897, for band
    I:BGi (Faldone 41, n. 440.58) [Anesa]
MS  I:OS (Mss.B.4239)

*Katty.* Mazurka (1892)
MS  band
    I:MAC (mss.37/30 bis) [autograph]

*Sul verone. Pensiero notturno* per Banda
EP  (Firenz, Lapini), for band
    I:BGi (Faldone 41, n. 439) [Anesa]

## De Marinis, Clodomiro

*Sinfonia Firenze*
EP   (Firenz, 1896)
        I:Mc (A.45.16.27)

## De Michelis, Cesare (1810–1867)

*Calde lagrime*. Marcia Funebre
EP   (Firenze, Lapini), 1896, for band
        I:BGi (Faldone 42, n. 446) [Anesa]

## Deola, Paolo

*Dixit* in B♭ (1845)
MS   2 voices, winds, organ
        I:Vsmc

Dixit in D (1847)
MS   TTB, winds, organ
        I:Vsmc

*Laudate pueri* in B♭ (1845)
MS   TTB, winds
        I:Vsmc

*Marcia*
MS   8 winds, organ
        I:Vsmc

## Devasini, Giuseppe (1822–1878)

*Messe solenne*
EP   (Milano,sd)
        I:Mc (A.45.12.35)
        This is an extraordinary, lengthy multi-movement work for band. The move-
        ments seem to precede or follow the traditional choral movements, which do not
        appear here]

## Diran, Adelaide

*Grande Polka* (composed for La Sultan Abdul-Meyjd)
EP   (Milano, 1852)
        I:Mc (A.45.13.4)

**Donelli, Benedetto (early nineteenth century professor at the Liceo Musicale Bologna)**

*Armonia* in F (1821)
MS  band (?)
    I:Bc

**Donizetti, Gaetano (1797–1848)**

*Domine ad adjuvandum* in C
MS  STB, 200-02, organ
    I:BGi (I.2a.E.16.78) [Anesa]

*Kyrie* in d minor
MS  STB, 200-02, org.
    I:BGi (I.1a.E.26.79) [Anesa]

*Kyrie* in C minor
MS  STB, 200-02
    I:BGi (I.1a.E.27) [Anesa]

*Marcia funebre* composta nell'anno 1842 in Milano per il rinomato scultore Pampeo Marchesi
EP  (Milan, sd) for TTB chorus and band
    I:Mc (A.45.13.6)
    US:DW

*Parisina* , Divertissement
EP  (London, 1882)
    GB:Lbm (h.1544.)

*Piccola Composizione* per strunenti a fiati e organo
MS  1000-321, organ [autograph score]
    I:BGi (I.1a.C.a)

*Qui tollis* in F
MS  T, solo clarinet, 200-12, organ
    I:BGi (I.1a.E.45.80) [Anesa]

*Qui tollis* in F
MS  T, solo clarinet, 2222-02, organ
    I:BGi (I.2a.E.51) [Anesa]

*Salve Regina.* in F
MS  STB, 200-221, bass
    I:BGi (I.2a.E.57.81) [Anesa]

*Sinfonia* a soli istromenti di fiato (18.17)
MS   1222-02
    I:BGi (I.2a.C.a/5) [autograph score]

Studio primo per Clarinetto (for Benigni)
MS   autograph score
    I:BGi (I.2a.C.c./3)

*Tantum ergo* in Eb
MS   T, 1002-22, st. bass
    I:BGi (I.2a.F/60) [autograph score]

## Donizetti, Giuseppe (1788–1856, brother to Gaetano Donizetti)

*Duetti* a due clarinetti (1821)
MS
    I:BGi (Faldone n. 10 [miscellanea non catalogata] .84) [Anesa]

## Dorn, Joseph

*Marcia Triplice Allianza* (1890)
MS   band
    I:Tr (Ob.240) [score]
    I:Tr (Ob.85) [parts]

## Dosi, Edelberto

*Attenti Marcia* (1881)
MS   band
    I:Tr (Ob.50)

## Elia, Giuseppe d'

*Inno di gloria e marcia*
MS   band
    I:Tr (ob.159)

## Erbin, Francesco

Passo doppio
MS   band
    I:Mc (Noseda)

**Ermagora, Fabio**

*Domini ad adjuvandun* (1856)
MS  3 voices, winds, organ
    I:Vsmc

*Inno di S. Antonio*
MS  3 voices, winds, organ
    I:Vsmc

*Salve regina*
MS  3 voices, winds, organ
    I:Vsme

*Tantum ergo*
MS  TB, winds, org
    I:Chioggia:Filippini

**Fabiani, Gaetano (1841–1904)**

*Amore e fratellanza*. Marcia sinfonica in A♭ (Oct. 25, 1891)
MS  band
    I:TE

**Faccini, Augusto**

*Cavatina* Originale per Banbardino and Banda
EP  (Milano, sd)
    I:Mc (A.45.13.21)

**Faccio, Francesso (1840–1891)**

*Overture Dramma. Maria Antonietta*
EP  (Milano, 1911)
    I:Mc (A.45.13.25)

**Fardini, G.**

*A Chiar di luna* (1892)
MS  band
    I:AGN

## Fassio, Giovanni

*Genova e Cristoforo Colombo*. Gran fantasia (1892)
MS   band
    I:Tr (ob. 161); US:DW

4 *Souvenir* (marches: Alessandria, Costantinopoli, Pietroburgo, Berlino)
MS   band
    I:Tr (ob. 201)

## Fattorini, ?

*Cavatina* per genis e banda
MS   horns and band
    I:FEM

## Fedeli, Pietro (b. 1785)

*Adagio marcia* in C
MS   21-02, organ
    I:Vsmc

*Ecce nuns*
MS   3 voices, clarinets and horns
    I:Vsmc

*Salve Regina* in C
MS   B, winds, org.
    I:Vsmc

## Ferradini, Mario

*Festa al villaggio*. Fantasia sinfonica
EP   (Firenz, Lapini), 1898, for band
    I:BGi (Faldone 48, n. 518) [Anesa]

*Pro rege*, Fantasia sinfonica
EP   (Firenz, 1897)
    I:Mc (A.45.17.3)
    I:BGi (Faldone 48, n. 517) [Anesa]

## Ferrante, Pasqual

*Pensiero sinfonico* (1895)
MS   band
    I:Tr (ob. 193); US:DW

**Fezzardi, Giovanni**

*Il Dialogo o sia Il Ritorno della Russia*
MS 3042-124
    I:OS (Mss.Mus.B.1150) [poetic note in Trombone 1]

*Marcia scritta espresamente per l'arrivo dei nuovi I stromenti di Medote* (1839)
MS band
    I:OS (Mss.Mus.B.3519)

*Marcia* (1838)
MS band
    I:OS (Mss.Mus.B.628)

*Serenata*
MS 3023-32
    I:OS (Mss.Mus.B.1149)

6 *Valzi*
MS band
    I:OS (Mss.Mus.B.473)

6 *Valzi* (for the dedication of a new town turbine)
MS band
    I:OS (Mss.Mus.B.3520)

**Filardi, Gregori**

*Marcia sinfonico*
MS band
    I:Messina-Univ.

**Filippi, Giuseppe (1836–1905)**

*Marcia funebre* per il transporto delle ceneri di G. Rossini da Parigi
MS band
    I:Fc (D.XI.3100)
MP www.whitwellbooks.com

**Filippa, Vittorio**

*Nozze in montegna.* Fantasia descrittiva per Banda.
EP (Firenze, Lapini), for band .
    I:BGi (Faldone 49, n. 529) [Anesa]

**Finali, ?**

> *Concerto* for clarinet
> MS clarinet, 11 winds
>> I:OS (Mss.Mus.B.3523)
> MP www.whitwellbooks.com

**Fiumi, Francesco**

> *Accorrete fedeli* (1886)
> MS 2 voices, bianche (?), band
>> I:RVE (337/XIII)

> *Maria che dolce nome* (1879)
> MS chorus, band
>> I:RVE (409/XIII)

> *Messa a piccola banda. e canto* in B♭
> MS
>> I:RVE (312/XIII)

> *Noi siam figlie di Maria* (1875)
> MS female chorus, band
>> I:RVE (408/XIII)

> *O Dolce Madre* (1881)
> MS 2 voices, band
>> I:RVE (372/XIII)

> *Ostella dei Vergine*
> MS chorus, band
>> I:RVE (406/XIII)

> *O Vergine pura* (1877)
> MS 2 voices, bianche, banda
>> I:RVE (377/XIII)

> *Salve o Maria Madre d'amore* (1873)
> MS chorus, band
>> I:RVE (407/XIII)

> *Su lodate o mari o monti* (1869)
> MS female chorus, band
>> I:RVE (404/XIII)

**Fontanelli, O.**

*Santa Tecla*. Marcia religiosa
EP   (Firenz, 1897)
   I:Mc (A.45.16.38)

**Fornasini, Nicola (1803–1861)**

*Sinfonia*
MS   1111-01
   I:Mc (Noseda)

**Foroni, Jacopo (1825–1858)**

*Sinfonia* in D Minori
EP   (Milano, 1901)
   I:Mc (A.45.14.22)
   This is a lengthy, one-movement work. The score says 'Instrumentazione di D. Barreca,' but the work looks like wind writing.

**Franceschini, Ernesto (b. 1837)**

*Notturno* (Ricordi concorso, 1892)
EP   (Milano, sd)
   I:Mc (A.45.14.24)

*Scherzo*
MS   solo cornet, tpt, trombone, euphoniun, band
   I:CRE

**Franchetti, Alberto (1860–1942)**

*Nella foresta nera*. Impressione sinfonica
EP   (Milano, 1911)
   I:Mc (A.45.15.14)

**Frattesi, Costantino**

*Quartet* in F
MS   31-
   I:Ria (Ms. 732)

### Frontini, Martino (1827–1909)

*Caccia al daino*. Fantasia sinfonica
MS  band
    I:Tr (ob. 71)

### Frosali, Giovanni Battista (d. 1924)

*Giotto*. Sinfonia descrittiva
EP  Firenze, Lapini, for band
    I:BGi (Faldone 50, n. 552) [Anesa]

### Fumagalli, Disna (1826–1893, Professor at the Milano Conservatoire)

*Alla tomba dei grandi, gran marcia funebre* (for the Nat. Guard in Torino)
EP  (Milano, 1859)
    I:Mc (B. 25-h-231-3/XVII)
    I:Mc (A.45.15.16) [another copy]
    This is an outstanding score for large band.

### Fumagalli, Polibio (1830–1901)

*Sestetto*, Op. 32
MS  1122-01
    I:BGi (xxx.656.11108)

### Furriel, Alfonso

*L'Alieanza*. Fantasia sinfonica
MS  band
    I:Tr (ob. 303)

### Galli, Amintore (1845–1919)

*Miserere* in d minor
MS  3 voices, 1020-12, timpani, organ
    I:BGc (Fald. 51)

### Gallo, Domenico (1730–1768)

*Magnificat* in Bb
MS  3 voices, winds, organ
    I:Vnm (Cod. It. IV .1438=11590)

**Gallo, Vincenzo**

*Piccola Sinfonia* per Banda (1884)
MS  band
    I:BAR (F.G.A.351) [original rescoring by the composer of an earlier symphony
    for orchestra]
    I:BAR (F.G.A.257) [original version]
MP  www.whitwellbooks.com

**Gambaro, Giovanni Battista (ca. 1780–1825, lived in Paris after 1812)**

*Quartet* in C
MS  1011-01
    I:Gl (SS.A.2.6)

*Quartet* Secondo in D
MS  1011-01
    I:Gl (SS.A.2.6)

**Gamberale, F.**

*Aria del Giovedi Santo* (1900)
MS  brass band
    I:AGN

**Gargiulo, ?**

*La Corona d'Italia*. Marcia trionfale
MS  band
    I:Tr (ob. 251)

**Gatti, Domenico (1816–1891)**

*Concerto originale* per cornetta e trombone
MS  band
    I:Leffe (Raccolta privata Pezzoli) [Anesa]

*La Dora*. cavatina Fantastica
MS  band
    I:FEM

*Valzer fantastico* per clarinetto
MS  band
    I:Leffe (Raccolta privata Pezzoli) [Anesa]

## Gherardeschi, Gherardo

*Marcia*
MS  band
> I:PS (B.193/2) [incomplete score]

*Messa*
MS  TTB, band
> I:PS (B.191/1)

## Gherardeschi, Luigi (1791–1871)

*Pastorale* (for the evening of S. Natale) (1817)
MS  band
> I:PS (B. 228 ,4) [also lots of church works for small ensembles of winds]

## Ghiti, G.

*Pietro Micca*. Ballo stor ico
MS  large band
> I:OS (Mss.Mus.B.3604)
> I:OS (Mss.Mus.B.1585) [one clarinet part only]

## Giorgi, Carlo

*Marcia funebre*
EP  (Milano, 1895)
> I:Mc (A.45.17.40)
> This is a good work with smaller instrumentation.

## Giorza, Paolo (1832–1914)

*Cleopatra, gran marcia funebre*
EP  (Milano, sd)
> I:Mc (A.45.17.49)

## Giudici, Eugenio (b. 1874)

*La fuga degli amanti*. Sinfonia descrittiva (1899)
MS  band, 35-page score
> I:BGi (Fondo Eugenio Giudici) [Anesa]

*Novelletta autunnale* (1899)
MS  band, 8 page score
> I:BGi (Fondo Eugenio Giudici) [Anesa]

*Preludio sinfonico festoso*
MS  band, 30-page score
    I:BGi (Fondo Eugenio Giudici) [Anesa]

## Grasso, F. P.

*Ottetto* in F minor per instrunenti ad ancia
EP  (Firenze, sd)
    I:Mc (A.45.18.19)

## Grazzini, Reginaldo (1848–1906)

*Marcia solenne*
EP  (Firenze, Lapini), 1896, band
    I:BGi (Faldone 55, n. 632) [Anesa]

## Greggiati, Giuseppe (1793–1866)

*Christe* in C
MS  T, 20-02, org.
    I:OS (Mss.Mus.B.383)

## Guarreri, Andrea

*Sestetto*
MS  1110-1011
    I:Gl (Sc.126)

## Guidi, Lorenzo

*Benedictus* (1853)
MS  3 voices, bsns, trombones
    I:Lucca-Ardl. del Crocifisro (A.10)

## Hugues, Luigi (1836–1913)

*Allegro Scherzoso*, intermezzo del Quintetto in Re, Op. 92
EP  (Millano, 1883)
    GB:Lbm (h.2140.j.[15.])

## Impallomeni, Gaetano (1841–1908)

*Omaggio al compianto* … Vittorio Emanuele II (1878) Marcia ftmebre
MS  band
    I:Tr (ob.17)

### Inico, Carlo (1863–1947)

*Elegia per Banda* (1890)
MS   band
    I:Tr (ob.163)

### Jommi, Alfonso

*Sinfonia — Italiana*
EP   (Firenze, 1898), band
    I:Mc (A.45.16.25)
    I:Mc (A.45.16.40) [another copy]
    I:BGi (Faldone 88, n. 811) [Anesa]

### Leto, Antonio

*E'salvo il re.* Inno-Marcia
MS   band
    I:Tr (ob.212)

### Lucchini, P.

*Kyrie e Gloria* in F
MS   2 voices, winds, organ
    I:Vsmc

### Luigini, ?

*Concerto* for bassoon e banda
MS   Bsn,band
    I:OS (mss.mus.B.3693)

### Mabellini, Teodulo (1817–1897)

*Fantasia* per banda
MS
    I:FAN (SV.15)

*Gran Fantasia*
MS   101-211
    I:FAN (XV.18)

*Gran Fantasia*
MS   1010-111
    I:FAN (XV.17)

*Gran Quintetto di concerto*
MS  1010-111
    I:FAN (SV.16)

2 *Marcie*
MS  band
    I:FAN (XV.14.)

## Magaldi, Vito

*Inno*
MS  voice and band
    I:Tr (ob.353)

## Magrini, Antonio

*Armonie*
MS  2001-02, tinpani, 2 viole
    I:Fc (D.X.382-389)

## Malerbi, Giuseppe (1771–1849, the teacher of Rossini)

2 *Allegro*
MS  winds
    I:Lugo-Istit.Mus. (Malerbi A.288, 289)

*Allegro con spirito*
MS
    I:Lugo-Istit.Mus. (Malerbi A.587)

*Allegro spiritoso*
MS
    I:Lugo-Istit.Mus. (Malerbi A.614)

*Andante*
MS  voice and winds
    I:Lugo-Istit.Mus. (Malerbi A.613)

## Maltoni, Domenico (1866–1937)

*Festa comunale*, Capriccio
EP  (Milano, sd) for solo trumpet and band
    I:Mc (A.4S.21.1)

## Manente, Giuseppe (1878–1941)

*Antico e moderno Sinfonia*
EP   (Firenze, 1896)
     I:Mc (A.45.16.36)
     I:BGi (Faldone 95, n. 902.67) [Anesa]

*Marcia religiosa*
EP   (Milano, sd)
     I:Mc (A.45.21.15)

*Marcia trionfale*
EP   (Firenze, Lapini), 1898, band
     I:BGi (Faldone 95, n. 901) [Anesa]

*Meditation religiuse*
EP   (Milano, 1899)
     I:Mc (A.45.21.20)

*Marcia religiosa* (miracolo eucaristico)
EP   (Milano, sd)
     I:Mc (A.45.21.16)

## Manente, Liberio (father of the previous composer)

*Fantasia*
MS   band
     I:Tr (ob.260)

## Maraseco, Giuseppe (1860–1930)

*Il corteggio*. Marcia Trionfale
EP   (Firenze, Lapini), 1898, band
     I:BGi (Faldone 95, n. 905) [Anesa]

## Marchetti, Luigi (b. 1848)

*Marcia Reale* [arr. for 400 players for a royal passage in 1878]
MS   band
     I:Tr (ob.238)

## Mariani, Giuseppe

*Elegia funebre*
EP   (Milano, 1900)
     I:Mc (A.45 .22 .23)

**Marro, Tammaso**

*Quintetto* in F
MS  21-02
    I:Tf (10.1.19.4)

**Marsand, Luigi**

*Inno* in G
MS  3 voices, winds, organ
    I:Vsmc

**Martelli, Bartolomeo**

*Litanie* in D
MS  TTB, clarini, corni, oboe
    I:REm (Mus. Sacra LXVII-14 bis)

**Marti, Esteban (pupil of Massenet)**

*Au Trianon*, Valse Lente Louis XV
EP  (Milano-Paris, 1898)
    I:Mc (A.45.23.3)

**Martinelli, Pietro**

*Nel cimitero*. Marcia funebre
MS  band
    I:Leffe(Raccolta privata Pezzoli) [Anesa]

**Martucci, Giuseppe (1856–1909)**

*Notturno* in sol bemolle
EP  (Milano, 1911)
    I:Mc (A.45.23.8)

**Marzo, Simone**

*Il Canto nazionale*
MS  singers and band
    I:Tr (ob. 378)

## Masutto, Renzo (b. 1858)

*Preludio sinfonico* 'Saluto alla Patria di Donizetti'
EP   (Firenze, Lapini) , 1890, band
  I:BGi (Faldone 100, n. 937.68) [Anesa]

## Matacena, Sebastiano

*L' Eroica* ... Fantasia militaire (1866)
MS   Inf. band, 4 Fanfare bands, cavalry band
  I:Tr (ob.250)

## Mattiozzi, Rodolfo (1832–1875)

*Canto marziale dei soldati italiani* (band and chorus)
EP   (Firenze, Lapini), band
  I:BGi (Faldone 210, n. 2893.70) [Anesa]

## Mayr, Johann Simon (1763–1845)

*Alma Redemptoris* in B♭
MS   T solo, 222-021, organ
  I:BGc (Mayr.Faldone 15) [Anesa]

*Ave maris stella* in F
MS   4 Voice, winds
  I:BGc (Mayr.Faldone 16) [Anesa]

*Averte faciem* in F
MS   S, 21-02
  I:BGc (Mayr.Faldone 216) [Anesa]

*Bagatella* a tre [?]
MS   1011-01
  I:Mc (Noseda)

*Credo* in C 'di Novara'
MS   piccolo, E♭ cl, 3 trombones, serpent, contrabsn
  I:BGc (Mayr. Faldone 87) [Anesa]

*Cum sancto spiritu* in C
MS   STB, 20-121, timpani, organ
  I:BGi (992.D.107)

*Dixit* in B♭
MS   STB, 20-02
  I:BGi (997.D.112)

*Domine ad adjuvandum, e Magnificat* in C
MS  TTB, 1020-121, organ
    I:BGc (Mayr.Faldone 139) [Anesa]

*Eja mater* in F
MS  SATB, 200-12, cello
    I:BGi (Mayr.Faldone 112, n. 998) [Anesa]

*Graduale* per S. Luigi in F
MS  SSS, 1021-121, organ
    I:BGc (Mayr.Faldone 72) [Anesa]

*Laudamus*
MS  TB, 2000-12, organ, bc
    I:BGi (1019A)

*Laudate Dominun* in E♭
MS  SATB, 2122-122, timpani, organ
    I:BGc (Mayr.Faldone 8) [Anesa]

*Lievi aurette*
MS  T, 2000-, basset horn, harp
    I:BGi (Mayr 323.19) [autograph score]

*Marcia*
MS  3111-12, perc.
    I:BGc (Mayr 252.16)

*Marcia lugubre* in C minor
MS  2222-241, 2 basset horns, contrabsn, timpani, bass drum
    I:BGc (Mayr.Faldone 47) [Anesa]

*Messa* a stromenti da fiato in E♭
MS  1111-121, organ timpani
    I:BGc (Mayr 96.1)
    This is apparently only the Kyrie and Gloria in autograph score. Another version
    exists for full orchestra.

*Messa da Requiem* in E♭
MS  SATB, 1021-121, timpani, organ
    I:BGc (Mayr.Faldone 36) [Anesa]

*Miserere* (1845)
MS  4 voices, 20-121, timpani
    I:BGi (1022.A.1)
    I:BGc (Mayr.Fald.214) [this copy is in the hand of Donizetti]

4 *Notturni* per nove instrum.
MS 1022-121
    I:BGi (XXIV.I.576.9751)

*O quam tristis*
MS solo TT, trumpet or oboe, 21-02, viola (talia?)
    I:BGi (Mayr.23.3) [autograph score]

*O Salutaris hostia*
MS TTB, 1111-111, cb
    I:BGc (Mayr.Faldone 15) [autograph]

*O Salutaris hostia*
MS SSSAAA., -121, organ
    I:BGc (Mayr.Faldone 15)

*O Salutaris hostia*
MS TTTB, 111-111, cb
    I:BGc (Mayr.Faldone 15)

*Ottetto* in D
MS 221-12
    I:BGi (Mayr.317.3) [autograph]

*Ottetto*
MS 1021-01, 2 bassi
    I:BGi (Mayr.314.25.3)

*Pange lingua* in C
MS SATB, 212-02
    I:BGc (Mayr.Faldone 16) [Anesa]

*Pange lingua* in C
MS 4 voices, 211-02
    I:BGc (Mayr.16.37)

*Salve Regina* in C
MS SB, 202-02, organ
    I:BGc (Mayr.Faldone 307) [Anesa]

*Salve regina* (1798)
MS S, 201-02, organ
    I:Vc (Correr 52-60) [autograph score]

7 *Sestetti per fiati* [elsewhere: Divertimento in E♭]
MS 121-02, basso
    I:BGc (Mayr.252.16) [autograph score]

*Sestetto*
MS  22-02
    I:BGc (Mayr.319.6)

2 *Settimini*
MS  22-03
    I:BGc (Mayr.302.16)

*Settimino*
MS  202-02, basset horn
    I:BGc (Mayr.319.5)

N.7 *Alla francese*
MS  220-04
    I:BGc (Mayr.299.6)

*Sicut erat* in B♭
MS  STB, 100-02
    I:BGi (Mayr.Faldone 48, n. 1045) [Anesa]

8 *Sonate*
MS  21-02, basset horn
    I:BGc (Mayr.306.02)

2 *Sonate*
MS  21-02, basset horn, viola (talia?)
    I:BGc (Mayr.306.13)

*Stabat mater* in F
MS  SS, 21-02
    I:BGc (Mayr.16.38)
    I:BGc (Mayr.Faldone 16) [Anesa]

*Stabat mater* in G
MS  SATB, 201-02
    I:BGc (Mayr.16.40)
    I:BGc (Mayr.Faldone 16) [Anesa]

*Suonate* a sei istrumenti
MS  21-02, 2 basset horns
    I:BGc (Mayr.Faldone 306) [Anesa]

*Te Joseph celebrent.*
MS  STB, 100-02
    I:BGc (Mayr.16.41)

*Viderunt te aqua*, per benedizione di campane, in D
MS  STB, 20-021, organ
    I:BGc (Mayr.Faldone 11) [Anesa]

## Mazzorin, Michele

*Sanctus* (1830)
MS  TTB, 11 winds
    I:Chiogga:Filippani

## Menghetti, Giuseppe (1784–1806)

*Tre Sinfonie* per Banda (Argentina, Una Notte per Mere, and Marcia funebre
MS  band
    I:FAN (Federici 285, i) [score and parts]

## Mercadante, Saverio (1795–1870)

*Ballabile*, 1842
MS  2222-243, perc
    BRD:Sl (H.B.XVII, Nr. 747)

*Inno a Vittorio Emanuelle re d'Italia*, per festa dello Statuto
MS  chorus, orchestra & band
    I:Bc

*Gran marcia reale* per Bande e fanfarre mil. (dedicated to the King of Greece)
MS  band
    I:Ria (Ms. 364)

## Micrio, Salvatore

*March Amore e speranze* (1881)
MS  band
    I:Tr (ob.285)

## Miglio, Pietro

*La Mostra di Napoli*. Overture
MS  band, score
    I:Tr (ob.64)

## Migliorini, ?

*Gratitudine March*
MS  band
    I:FEM

## Mililotti, Giuseppe (1828-1883, conductor, National Guard Band of Rome)

*L' Europa innanzi la salma de Vittorio Emanuele II.* Marcia funebre per gran Banda Mil. (1878)
MS  band, autograph score
    I:Tr (ob.192)

*Una Lacrima sulla tomba.* Elegia sinfonica (1870)
MS  band
    I:Rrostirolla (Ms.Mus.41, c. 1-10)

## Mingozzi, Giuseppe

*Aria*
MS  7 winds
    I:Fc (D.V.508)

## Mondrone, Pasqual

*Capriccio sinfonico* (1892)
MS  band
    I:Tr (ob.4)

## Monina [here Manina], Fortunato

*Tantum ergo* in G
MS  3 voices, winds, organ
    I:Vsmc

## Montanari, Angelo

*Pensieri lugubri*
EP  (Firenze, sd)
    I:Mc (A.45.26.19)

## Montebagnoli, Sante

*Serenata*
MS  1021-021
    I:OS (mss.mus.B.3821)

## Morlacchi, Francesco (1784–1841)

*Francesca da Rimini*, Sinfonia
EP   (Milano, 1910)
    I:Mc (A.45.27.7)

## Mutor, Giuseppe

*Marcia funebre*
MS
    I:Rrostirolla (Ms.Mus.164)

## Napoli, Giovanni di'

*Preludio sinfonico* in Ab
MS   cavalry band
    I:PLoon (D.13)

## Napolitano, Pasquale

*Ode alla regina* (1893)
MS   band
    I:Tr (Ob. 362)

## Natale, Luigi

*Polka*
MS   band
    I:Tr (Ob. 320)

## Nau, Francesco

*Andante* in C; *Valzer* in F
MS   21-12
    I:OS (Mss.Mus.B.2403)

## Necchi, Francesco

*Magnificat* in F
MS   STB, 101-1, bass
    I:Bsf

**Neri, ?**

*Fantasia on Otello* (Verdi)
MS band
    I:FEM

**Neri, Giuseppe**

*Elena.* Mazurka
MS band
    I:Tr (Ob. 69)

**Nicolini, Giuseppe (1762–1842)**

*Cantata* (1815)
MS voices, 2122-12, celli
    I:Vmarcello (cod. 213)

**Nini, Alessandro (1805–1880)**

*Stabat mater per processione* in Eb
MS SATTBB, 2122-223, timpani
    I:BGi (Fondo Cappella Basilica S. Maria Maggiore, Faldone 228, n. 784) [Anesa]

**Nipel, Francesco**

*La Rocca eli Bellagio.* Marcia
MS band
    I:Mc (Noseda)

**Nobili, Sllvio**

*Il Dolore.* Marcia funebre
MS band
    I:Tr (Ob. 19)

**Nocentini, Domenico (1848–1924)**

*Santa Marta.* Marcia religiosa
MS band
    I:Leffe(Raccolta privata Pezzoli) [Anesa]

### Novaro, Michele (1818–1885)

*Inno di Mameli*
MS  band
    I:FEM

### Nutti, Attilio

*Sinfonia* per Orchestra e Banda
MS  band and orchestra
    I:Prato Scuola Comunale

### Nutti, Dante

*Il Risorgimento Italiano*. Marcia
MS  band
    I:Prato Scuola Comunale

*Voluttuosa*. Mazurka
MS  band
    I:Prato Scuola Comunale

### Olivieri, Alessio

*Inno di Garibaldi*.
MS  band
    I:FEM

### Orgalesi, Tamaso

*Marcia funebre*
MS  band
    I:Gandino(Archivio Parrocchiale)

### Orlandi, ?

*Chiome nere*. Valzer
MS  band
    I:FEM

### Orsi d', ?

*La Sardegnola March*
MS  band
    I:FEM

## Pacini, Giovanni (1796–1867)

*Cavatina*
EP   (London, 1860, in Boose's supplemental military Journal, Nr. 182)
   GB:Lbm (h.1544.)

*Concertone* per Oboe, Clar, Tranba, & Trombone in E♭
MS   band
   I:Ls (B.114)

*Concertone* in Re
MS   band
   I:Ls (B.90)
   I:Ls (B.98) [another score]
   I:Ls (B.108) [parts]

*Gran Concertone* per f1ute, clarinet, corno, tromba, & trombone in B♭
MS   band
   I:Ls (B.46)
   I:Ls (B.1181) [ridotto per Banda in D]

*Credo* per fanfara in E♭
MS   band
   I:Ls (B.75)

## Paer, Ferdinando (1771–1839)

*La Camila*
MS   eight-part Harmoniemusik
   I:BGc (Mayr.E.1.7)

*La Cantata per il Natale* (Oratorio)
MS   eight-part Harmoniemusik
   I:Fc (D.V.506)

## Paganelli, Giovanni

*Marcia eroica*
MS
   I:Ria (Ms.376) [may be early twentieth century]

## Paganini, Ercole (1770–1825)

*Olimpia*
MS   eight-part Harmoniemusik
   I:Fc (D.V.572)

## Palazzi, Ercolo

*Pezzi d'opera*
MS   nine winds
    I:COR

## Palmerini, Luigi (1768–1842)

*Alma Redemtoris* (1803)
MS   TTB, winds
    I:LU (Malerbi.C.35)

## Palmieri, Giuseppe

*Il Risorgimento nazionale.* Gran marcia trionfale
MS   band
    I:Tr (Ob. 170)

## Pangaldi, ?

*Mazurca*
MS   band
    I:FEM

## Pannocchia, U.

*Lealta Marcia*
MS   band
    I:Tr (Ob. 256)

## Pansi, ?

*Messa* per Organo o Piccola Banda
MS
    I:RVE (515/XIII)

## Pantaleo, Luigi

*L'Eco d'Italia.* Polka
MS   band
    I:Tr (Ob. 316)

## Panuccio, Domenico

*Inno a sua maesta Umberto I* (1881)
MS   band
    I:Tr (Ob. 109)

## Paravicini, ?

*Melodia del lago*. Valzer
MS  band
    I:FEM

*Pere moscatelle*. Valzer
MS  band
    I:FEM

*Il Postiglione*. Galop
MS  band
    I:FEM

*Le Rose*. Valzer
MS  band
    I:FEM

## Parisi, Filippo

*Andante per Armonia*. Elevazione (1848)
MS  band
    I:OS (Ms.Mus.B.4791)

## Parisi, Vittorio

*Italia*. Fantasia caratteristica
MS  band
    I:Tr (Ob. 62)

## Parmegiani, Gaetano

*Sinfonia originale* (Bologna, 1896)
MS  band
    I:Tr (ob. 48)
MP  www.whitwellbooks.com

## Pasini, Timoteo (d. 1889)

*Ave Maris Stella* in E♭
MS  chorus and band
    I:RVE (517/XIII)

*Magnificat* in B♭
MS  chorus and band
    I:RVE (519/XIII)

*Vespro; Domine; Dixit; Laudate; Magnificat*
MS chorus and band
    I:RVE (521/XIII)
    I:RVE (523/XIII) [related manuscripts]

*Vespro; Domini; Dixit*
MS chorus and band
    I:RVE (522/XIII)

## Pedrotti, Carlo (1817–1892)

*Con te tracorrere*
EP (London, 1883)
    GB:Lbm (h.1549.)

*Fiorini Sinfonica*
EP (Milano, 1908)
    I:Mc (A.45.28.14)
    This is a one-movement work with many sections; the 36 page score says 'instr. by Antonio Paiola.'

## Pellarin, Giuseppe (1815–1865)

*Confitebor* in B♭
MS 3 voices, winds, organ
    I:Vsmc

*Tantum ergo* in B♭ (1836)
MS T, horns, clarinets, organ
    I:Vsmc

## Pellegrini, Giulio (1800–1858)

*Marcia trionfale*
MS band
    I:Tr (ob.108)

## Perolini, Eugenio (1829–1907)

*Medici alla battaglia di Primolano Duplice sinfonia* a due bande. (dedicated to Napoleone III)
MS 2 bands
    I:Mc (A.45.29.3)
    This is a massive work for two bands. The score has very faint staff lines, written with a very fine pen. Huge pages.

## Peroni, Alessandro (1874–1964)

*Marcia funebre*
EP   (Milano, 1904)
    I:Mc (A.45.29.30)

*Intermezzo elegiaco*
EP   (Milano, 1905)
    I:Mc (A.45.29.26); US:DW

*Overture romantique*
EP   (Milano, 1913)
    I:Mc (A.45 .29 .28); US:DW

*La victorieuse Overture*
EP   (Milano, 1907)
    I:Mc (A.45.29.31)

## Perosi, Lorenzo (b. 1872)

*La passione eli Cristo* secondo S. Marco. Trilogia sacra. Preludio Parte III.
EP   (Milano, 1900)
    I:Mc (A.45.29.32)

*La resurrezione di Lazzaro*, Oratorio. Preluldio sunto della prima parte e finale II.
EP   (Milano, 1900)
    I:Mc (A.45.29.33)

## Perotta, G.

*Emilia*. Sinfonia per Banda
MS  band
    I:LU

## Perotti, ?

*Fiori Valzer*
MS  band
    I:MAC (Ms.Mus.47/27b)

## Petrali, Vincenzo, 1832-1889

*A Grande Velocita*. Galop (1867)
MS  band
    I:BGc (Fald.65)

*L'Alloggio militaire,* per carnevale 1878–1879
MS   band
    I:BGc (Mayr.65.23)

*Bizzarria.* Galop
MS   band
    I:BGc (Fald. 65)

*Centomila Frnachi di rendita.* Valzer (1865)
MS   band
    I:CRE

*'Chi me Vuole?'* Mazurka
MS   band
    I:BGc (Fald.65)

*'Come me chiami'*: Polka
MS   band
    I:BGc (Fald. 65)

*Estasi amorosa.* Mazurka
MS   band
    I:BGc (Mayr.65.42)

*Foglie disperse.* Valzer (1860)
MS   band
    I:CRE

*Invito alla danza.* Valzer (1861)
MS   band
    I:CRE

*Magnificat* (1870)
MS   SATB, winds, organ
    I:BGi (xxxv.654.11081)

*Manilla.* Schottish
MS   band
    I:BGc (Fald.65)

*Mazurka*
MS   band
    I:BGc (Fald.65)

*Pot-pourri on Lucia di Lammermoor* (Donizetti)
MS   band
    I:CRE

*Pot-pourri on Poliuto* (Donizetti)
MS band
  :CRE

*Il Rostiglione di Brunn* (1866)
MS band
    I:CRE

*Rimanbranze* [Fantasia] dalla 'Contessa d' Arnalfi' (1871)
MS band
    I:CRE

*Rimanbranze dalla Norma* (Bellini)
MS band
    I:CRE

*Scacciapensieri*. Galop
MS band
    I:CRE

*Souvenir dell' opera Don Carlos* (Verdi)
MS band
    I:CRE

*Souvenir dell' opera Marta* (Flotow)
MS band
    I:CRE

*Triade*. Polka
MS band
    I:BGc (Fald.65)

*Zibaldone*. Galop
MS band
    I:BGc (Fald.65)

## Petrella, Errico (1813–1877)

*Jone,* marcia funebre
EP  (Milano, 1905)
    I:Mc (A.45.30.1)
    I:Mc (A.45.30.2) [another copy]

## Pezzoli, Antonio (1842–1908)

The following compositions are found in I:Leffe (Raccolta private Pezzoli) as reported by Anesa.

*Duettino* (Qui tollis) in F
MS   TB, 1021-222, bass

*Il ritorno*. Pezzo d'assiane per banda (1891)
MS   band

*Memoria di Sacile*. Divertimento per banda
MS   band

*Ricordo alIa stella*. Fantasia (1899)
MS   band

## Pezzoli, Giovanni (1870–1934)

The following compositions are found in I:Leffe (Raccolta private Pezzoli) as reported by Anesa.

*Domine ad adjuvandum* in F (1895)
MS   1021-222, bombardone, bass

*Kyrie* (1892) in F minor
MS   TTBB, 2020-122, bass, timpani

## Pezzoli, Giuseppe (1831–1908)

The following compositions are found in I:Leffe (Raccolta private Pezzoli) as reported by Anesa.

*Credo* in B♭
MS   TTB, 1011-1, bombardone

*Credo* in F
MS   TTBB, 2020-222, bombardone, bass, timpani

*Dixit Dominus* in E♭ (1890)
MS   TTB, 1010-, bass

*Domine ad adjuvandum* in F
MS   TTB, 10-001

*Domine Deus* (1889) in B♭
MS   TTB, solo cl, 1020-222, oficleide

*Fede ed amore*. Fantasia per banda.
MS  band

*Inno* (Iste confessor o Ave Maris Stella) in E♭
MS  TTBB, 1020-122, timpani

*Kyrie* in C
MS  TTBB, 20-123, bombardone, 2 fliscorno

Laudamus in D
MS  T, solo fl, 20-123, bombardone, bass, piccolo

*Laudate pueri Dominum* in B♭
MS  TTBB, solo cl, 1011-111, bombardone, timp

*Magnificat* in F
MS  TTB, 1010-

*Pange lingua* in E♭
MS  TTBB, 2020-122, bombardino, bassi, perc, organ, fliscorno

*Qui tollis* in C minor
MS  B, chorus, solo tpt, 1020-221, bombardone, bass, piccolo

*Sanctus, Benedictus e Angus Dei* in B♭
MS  [voices missing?], 1021-222, oficleide, bass

*Stabat Mater* Nr. 1 in F (1894)
MS  TTBB, 1120-123, bombardone, piccolo

*Stabat Mater* Nr. 2 in F minor
MS  TTBB, 1120-223, piccolo, oficleide

*Stabat Mater* in F minor (1887)
MS  TTBB, 2020-222, perc, bomb., 2 fliscorno, organ

## Picchianti, Luigi (1786–1864)

*Notturno*
MS  1100-01, chitarra
    I:Fc (D.X.102-105)

## Pieroni, Leopoldo (b. 1847)

*Inno alla memoria del Padre della Patria Vittorio Emanule II*
MS
    I:Tr (Ob.337) [score for band]

## Pigna, Alessandro

*Scintille celesti*
EP   (Milano, sd)
    I:Mc (A.45.30.5)

## Pisapia, Raffaele

*Scene d'un villaggio*
EP   (Firenze, Lapini), 1898, for band
    I:BGi (Faldone 120, n. 1156) [Anesa]

## Poggi, Augusto

*Corteggio trionfale*
MS   band
    I:Ria (Ms.228)

## Ponchielli, Amilcare (1834–1886)

The following are original compositions for band. The catalog numbers given below are those found in Sirch, *Catalogo Thematico*.

*Sinfonia* in F minor, Op. 106 (ca. 1850)
MS   band
    I:CR (Ponchielli 129) [autograph score]
    In I:Mc there is an alternative set of orchestral parts, in G minor, but no score, in the composer's hand.
MP   www.whitwellbooks.com

*Sinfonia* in B♭ minor
MS   band
    I:CR (Ponchielli 123) [autograph score]
MP   www.whitwellbooks.com

*Fantasia Militare*, Op. 116 (ca. 1858)
MS   band
    I:Mc (T.ii.64/5)
EP   Ricordi, sd
    I:Mc (Riserva Mus. E-150/16 Banda)
    US:DW (1134)

*Capriccio sull'Opera 'Roberto il Diavolo'* (Meyerbeer), Op. 117 (1862)
MS   band
    I:CR (Ponchielli 303)

*Marcia* N. 9, in B♭, (1864), Op. 118
MS  band
    I:CR (Ponchiel1i 344)
    US:DW

(Marcia) *Viva Il Re* in A♭, Op. 119 (1862–1864)
MS  band
    I:Tr (ob.32)
    US:DW (1140)

*Marcia* N. 3, in A♭, Op. 120 (1865)
MS  band
    I:CR (Ponchielli 361)

*Marcia Funebre* per Amilcare Ponchielli, in B♭ minor, Op. 121 (1865)
MS  band
    I:CR (Ponchielli 133)

*Follie di Donna* (Valzer) in B♭b, Op. 122 (1866)
MS  band
    I:CR (Ponchielli 384)

*Concerto* for trumpet, in F, Op. 123 (ca. 1866)
MS  solo trumpet and band
    I:CR-Biblioteca Statale (ms. civ. 76)
MP  www.whitwellbooks.com

*Principe Umberto Marcia*, in B♭, Op. 124 (1866)
MS  band
    I:CR-Biblioteca Statale (ms. civ. 90)
    US:DW

*Fantasia sul 'I due Foscari'* (Verdi), Op. 125 (1866)
MS  band
    I:CR (Ponchielli 395)

*Fantasia Originale* in B♭, Op. 126 (1866)
MS  band
    I:CR (Ponchielli 131)

*Ricordanze dell'Opera 'La Savojarda,'* Op. 127 (1866)
MS  band
    I:CR (Ponchielli 130)

*Per le esequie di Francesco Lucca* in B♭ Minor, Op. 112a (1866)
MS   band and orchestra
      I:CR–Biblioteca Statale (ms. civ. 87)
EP   (Milano, 1899)
      I:Mc (A.45.30.13)
      US:DW (1136)

*Gran Capriccio sul 'Rigoletto'* (Verdi), Op. 128 (1866)
MS   band
      I:CR (Ponchielli 286)

*L'Innamorata* (Mazurca) in B♭, Op. 129 (ca. 1866)
MS   band
      I:CR (Ponchielli 353)

*Lavinia* (Scottisch) in B♭, Op. 130 (ca. 1866)
MS   band
      I:CR (Ponchielli 350)

*Potpourri sull'Opera 'La Favorita'* (Donizetti), Op. 131 (dc. 1866)
MS   band
      I:CR (Ponchielli 310)

*Roma!* (Marcia) in E♭, Op. 132 (ca. 1866)
MS   band
      I:CR (Ponchielli 373)

*Seduzione Valzer* in E♭, Op. 133 (ca. 1866)
MS   band
      I:CR (Ponchielli 334)

*Ricordanze del Carnevale 1866*, Op. 134
MS   band
      I:CR (Ponchielli 346)

*Potpourri sull'Opera 'Faust'* (Gounod), Op. 135 (1867)
MS   band
      I:CR (Ponchielli 370)

*Il Colera*, Marcia funebre in B♭ Minor, Op. 136 (1867)
MS   band
      I:CR (Ponchielli 117)

*Ginevrina* (Scottisch) in F, Op. 137 (ca. 1867)
MS   band
      I:CR (Ponchielli 363)

*Marcia* N. 11 in A♭, Op. 138 (ca. 1867)
MS  band
    I:CR (Ponchielli 329)

*Potpourri sulla 'Gemna di Vergy'* (Donizetti), Op. 139 (1868)
MS  band
    I:CR (Ponchielli 316)

*Carnevale di Venezia* (15 Variations), Op. 140 (1868)
MS  band
    I:CR-Biblioteca Stattale (ms. civ. 91)
MP  www.whitwellbooks.com

*Lisa* (Polka) in F, Op. 141 (ca. 1868)
MS  band
    I:CR (Ponchielli 348)

*Mimy e Pipy* (due Scottisch), Op. 142 a-b (1869)
MS  band
    I:CR (Ponchielli 380)

*Potpourri sull'Opera 'Crispino e la Comare'* (Ricci), Op. 143 (1869)
MS  band
    I:CR (Ponchielli 293)

*Canto Greco* (10 Variations), Op. 144 (1869)
MS  band
    I:CR (Ponchielli 125)

*Marcia Funebre* N. 12 in E♭ Minor, Op. 145 (1869)
MS  band
    I:CR (Ponchielli 115)

*Fantasia su 'La Traviata,'* Op. 146 (1869)
MS  band
    I:CR (Ponchielli 282)

*Ricordanze dell'Opera 'Dinorah'* (Meyerbeer), Op. 147 (1869)
MS  band
    I:CR (Ponchielli 345)

*Sogni di Guerra* (Marcia) in E♭, Op. 148 (1869)
MS  band
    I:CR (Ponchielli 331)

*Reminiscenze dell' Opera 'Don Sebastiano'* (Donizetti), Op. 149 (1869)
MS   band
    I:CR (Ponchielli 301)

*Piazza Stradlivari* (Marcia) in E♭, Op. 150 (1870)
MS   band
    I:CR (Ponchielli 364)

*L'Eco del Castello* (Mazurca) in A♭, Op. 151 (1870)
MS   band
    I:CR (Ponchiell 336)

*Carmelita* (Mazurca) in B♭, Op. 152 (ca. 1871)
MS   band
    I:CR-Biblioteca Statale (ms. civ. 84)

*Volutta del Ballo* in E♭, Op. 154 (1872)
MS   band
    I:CR (Ponchielli 122)

*Concerto* per filcorno basso, Op. 155 (1872)
MS   band
    I:CR (Ponchielli 124)

*Una Follia a Roma* (Marcia) in E♭, Op. 156 (1872)
MS   band
    I:CR (Ponchielli 379)

*Per I Funerali di Alessandro Manzoni*, Op. 157 (ca. 1873)
MS   band
    I:Mr (T. ii.6418)
EP   (Ricordi, 1873)
    I:Mc (A.4S.30.11)
    US:DW (1133)

*Frenesia per Il Ballo* in B♭, Op. 158 (ca. 1873)
MS   band
    I:CR (Ponchielli 362)

*Il Gottardo, Inno trionfale*, Op. 159 (1882)
MS   for orchestra and band
    I:Mr (M. iv.15)

*Sulla Tomba di Garibaldi*, Elegia, Op. 160 (1882)
MS  band
    I:CR (Ponchielli 113)
EP  (Ricordi, 1882)
    I:Mc (Riserva Mus. 3-150-13)
MP  www.whitwellbooks.com

*Adele* (Valzer) in A♭, Op. 161
MS  band
    I:CR (Ponchielli 325)

*Adelina* (Polka) in E♭, Op. 162
MS  band
    I:CR (Ponchielli 339)

*Alla Memoria di mio Padre* (Marcia funebre), Op. 163 (ca. 1873)
EP  (Ricordi) 1873)
    I:Mc (A.45.30.13)
    US:DW (1136)

*L'Arrivo del Re* (Marcia) in A♭, Op. 164
MS  band
    I:CR (Ponchielli 375)

*Colpo d'Apoplessia*, Marcia funebre in C Minor, Op. 165
MS  band
    I:CR (Ponchielli 119)

*Democrazia* (Marcia) in E♭, Op. 166
MS  band
    I:CR (Ponchielli 330)

*Marcia* N. 4 in E♭, Op. 167
MS  band
    I:CR (Ponchielli 359)

*Marcia* N. 6 in E♭, Op. 168
MS  band
    I:CR (Ponchielli 326)

*Marcia* N. 7 in A♭, Op. 169
MS  band
    I:CR (Ponchielli 365)

*Marcia* N. 12 in F, Op. 170
MS  band
    I:CR (Ponchielli 337)

*Marcia* N. 13 in B♭, Op. 171
MS  band
    I:CR (Ponchielli 332)

*Marcia funebre* N. 1 in C Minor, Op. 172
MS  band
    I:CR (Ponchielli 121)

*Marcia funebre* N. 2 in B♭ Minor, Op. 173
MS  band
    I:CR (Ponchielli 120)

*Milano* (Marcia) in A♭, Op. 174
MS  band
    I:Gl (Sc. 30 n.n) [as *Marcia Trionfale*]
    US:DW (1707)

*Palestro* (Marcia) in E♭, Op. 175
MS  band
    I:CR (Ponchielli 374)

*Polka nel Ballo 'Il Viaggio della Luna,'* Op. 176
MS  band
    I:CR (Ponchielli 341)

*Principe Amedeo* (Marcia) in B♭, Op. 177
MS  band
    I:CR (Ponchielli 376)

*Ricordanze nell'Opera 'Luisa Miller'* (Verdi), Op. 178
MS  band
    I:CR-Biblioteca Statale (ms. civ. 56)

*Tabe Senile,* Marcia funebre N. 7, Op. 179
MS  band
    I:CR (Ponchielli 118)

*La Tassa Mobiliare* (Polka), Op. 180
MS  band
    I:CR (Ponchielli 352)

*Vittoria,* Marcia N. 8 in E♭, Op. 181
MS  band
    I:CR (Ponchielli 351)

*W L'Esposizione di Cremona*, Marcia in A♭, Op. 182
MS band
    I:CR (Ponchielli 284)
    There are also 78 transcriptions for band by this master composer, including numerous opera overtures and arias, dance works, and one anonymous *Concerto per Cornetto e banda*.

## Pontecchi, Egisto

*Inn all'adige* (1895)
MS chorus and band
    I:BGi (XXVIII.H.436.5455) [autograph score]

## Provesi, Ferdinand

*Dies Irae*
MS 3 voices, band
    I:CMGd (297) [incomplete]

## Puccini, Domenico (1771–1815)

*Christus* in D
MS 3 voices, winds
    I:Ls (c.20) [autograph score]

## Puccini, Giacomo (1858–1924)

*Inno* a Roma per Banda
MS band
    I:FEM [sc and pts]

*Da Suor Angelica*: Intermezzo per banda
MS
    I:FEM

## Pugni, Cesare (1802–1870)

*Serenata*
MS 1012-02, Eng. hn
    I:Mc (Da Camera Ms. 21/1)

## Rabitti-Sangiorgio, Giovanni Battista, 1797-1844

*Tantum ergo*
MS TT, 8 winds
    I:REm (Mus.Sacra XXXX.46) [autograph score]

*Tantum ergo* (1842)
MS   TT, winds
    I:REm (Mus.Sacra XXXX.47)

## Raimondi, Giovanni

*Marcia*
MS   22-022
    I:Ria (Ms.541)

## Ramagini, Domenico

*Messe brieve* (1808)
MS   4 voices, band
    I:Spello:S. Lorerrz; (54) [autograph score]

## Rambelli, Dario

*Preludio* per banda
MS
    I:Lugo:Trisi

## Rampezzotti, E.

*Le Canzoni del soldato*. March
EP   (London, 1886)
    GB:Lbm (h.1549.)

*Festa nazionale*. March
EP   (London, 1886)
    GB:Lbm (h.1549.)

*Fantasia, 'Folk-songs of Italy'*
EP   (London, 1889)
    GB:Lbm (h.1549.)

## Reali, Carlo

*Viva il Re! Marcia* (1883)
MS   band
    I:Tr (ob.104)

**Reali, Dante**

>*Marcia sovrana* (dedicated to Leone XIII)
>MS  band
>>I:Rvat (Mus.180)

**Reggiani, Ubaldo**

>*Marcia* (for the Queen of Italy)
>MS  band
>>I:Tr (ob.133)

**Reis, ?**

>*Kosaken 14.*
>MS  -Picoola Banda-
>>I:OS (Mus.Musiche.B.4819)

**Ricci, Niccolo**

>*Il Pianto d'Italia.* Marcia funebre a Vittorio Einanuele (1878)
>MS  band
>>I:Tr (Cp. 34/2)

**Ricordi, Giulio (1840–1912)**

>*Fermi.* Valzer (1857)
>MS  band
>>I:CRE

**Risi, ?**

>*Concerto* for Bombardino and band
>MS
>>I:FEM

>*Gran Duetto* per due Trombe e banda
>MS
>>I:FEM

>*Nido*, polca
>MS  band
>>I:FEM

**Rodella, ?**

*Galop*
MS  band
      I:OS (Ms.Mus.B.4003)

**Rolla, Alessandro (1757–1841)**

*Maestoso e Rondo* in D
MS  2042-22
      I:Tf (11.II.1-10)

**Rolla, Marco**

*Ottetto* ('per Carlo Paganelli, Milano, 1814')
MS  eight winds
      I:BRc (Pasini 29)

**Ramano, ?**

*Giorno di festa marcia*
MS  band
      I:FEM

**Rosi, ?**

*Pot-pourri da Carmen* (Bizet)
MS  band
      I:FEM

*Pot-pourri da La Gioconda e Mefistofele* (Ponchielli and Boito)
MS  band
      I:FEM

*Pot-pourri da Robert Le Diable* (Meyerbeer)
MS  band
      I:FEM

**Rossari, ?**

*Napoleone III. Marcia*
MS  band
      I:FEM

## Rossi, Isidoro (1813–1884)

*Amore* Valzer
MS band
    I:FEM

*Enrichetta*. Mazurca
MS band
    I:FEM

(3) *Quartets* (1870)
MS 2 E♭ trumpets, trombone, euphonium
    I:Mc (Da camera MS.22.7)

*Quintet* in E♭ (1868)
MS Soprano filicorno, trumpet, trombone, euphonium, tuba
    I:Mc (Da Camera MS.22.11)

*Quintet* in B♭
MS brass
    I:Mc (Da Camera MS.22.10)

*Sestetto concertato brillante* in E♭ (1869)
MS E♭ clar., B♭ clar., 2 trumpets, tenor horn, euphonium (and piano)
    I:Mc (Da Camera MS.22.8)

*Sestetto* in F
MS cornet, 2 tpts, 2 horns, trombone
    I:Mc (Da Camera MS.22.9)

(3) *Suonate*
MS 112-
    I:Mc (Da Camera MS.23.3)

*Tirolese Variata*
MS solo cornet and band
    I:FEM

*Trio*
MS three bassoons
    I:Mc (A.35.49/4)

(3) *Gran Trio* (1870)
MS soprano filicorno, trumpet, trombone
    I:Mc (Da Camera MS.22.13)

## Rossi, Lauro (1810–1885)

*Il domino nero*, sinfonia
EP   (Milano, 1907)
    I:Mc (A.45.35.20)

*Pezzo concertante* a 20
MS   for 3332-321, piccolo, contrabsn.
    I:Mc (Manoscritti 32/5)
    This is a massive but faint manuscript. The score appears unfinished, however, a set of
    parts is included!

## Rossini, Gioacchino (1792–1868)

*Marcia Pas-redoublé*
EP   (Milano, Ricordi, sd)
    I:Mc (Riserva Mus. e-150/14)
    This is the original edition of the march of the Abdul-Meyjd.

*L'Arrmonica cetra del nume.* Cantata
MS   SATB, TTB, 122l-02, harp
    DDR:Bds (Ms. auto. Microfilm)
    Composed for the namesday of the composer Zampieri (sic) in Bologna.

*La Corona d'Italia* per fanfare
MS
    I:PESc (Fondaz.Rossini) [autograph score]

3 *Marches for the duc d'Orleans* (called Pas redoublé)
MS   band
    I:Ria (Ms. 138)

*Marziale*
MS   6 winds, st. bass, organ, timpani
    I:Vsmc

*Theme & Variations*
MS   1011-01
    I:PESc (Fondaz. Rossini) [autograph]

*4 Walzer e 2 Contradanze*
MS   1001-, English horn
    I:OS (Mss.Musiche.B.2762)
    US:DW (1142)

## Rova, Giovanni

*O Jesu mi duclissime*. Motet (1847)
MS  3 voices, 5 winds
    I:Vsmc

*Tantum Ergo*
MS  3 voices, 6 winds
    I:Vsmc

## Ruggeri, Pietro

*Marcia funebre* (for Paganini)
EP   (Milano, 1853)
    I:Mc (A.45.36.10)

## Ruggi, Francesco (1767–1845)

*O sacrum convivium*. Antifona
MS  TTB, solo flute, 22-02, serpent
    I:Nc (Mus.relig.2063) [autograph score]

## Russo, Mariano

*Noi dei raggi delle stelle*
MS  chorus and band
    I:ACRz

## Sala, Eugenio

*Capriccio* per piccolo clarino & banda
MS
    I:Tr (ob.157) [score]

## Saluzzi, Francesco

[illegg] *lugubre* for winds
MS  band
    I:Ria (Ms.560)

## Sardei, Antonio

*Omaggio al re*. Sinfonia
MS  band
    I:Tr (ob.175) [score]

## Sarocchi, G.

*Inno del Doplavoro*
MS  band
    I:FEM

## Sassaroli, Vincenzo (late nineteenth century)

*Fantasia originale* per Banda
MS  band
    I:Gandino(Archivio Parrocchiale)

## Savazzini, Federico (b. 1830)

*Sinfonia* per Banda
MS  band
    I:Tr (ob. 247)
    US:DW

## Savoia, Paolo (b. 1820)

*Saluto alle nazioni* (Fantasia)
MS  band
    I:Tr (ov [ob?] 181/4)

## Scaglione, Antonio

*Credo* (1891)
MS  2 voices, band
    I:Messina-Universitaria

*Inno* (1894)
MS  2 voices, band
    I:Messina-Universitaria

*Vespro* (1884)
MS  2 voices, band
    I:Messina-Universitaria

## Schiavi, Corrado

*Andante religioso* (processional for Pio X)
MS  band
    I:Rvat (Mus.246)

*Grandioso*. Andante religioso (1904)
MS band
    I:Rvat (Mus.253)

## Sciacca, Vittoro

*Preludio funebre* (for Umberto I, 1900)
MS band
    I:Tr (ob.144)

## Sebastiani, Giuseppe

(2) *Passo doppio*
MS band
    I:Mc (Noseda)

*Tre Pezzi d'armonia*
MS 16 winds
    I:Nc

## Segneri, Vincenzo

*Il Ritorno*. Nuova Marcia
MS band
    I:Tr (Ob. 239)

## Seiller, A.

*Una Lagrima sulla tomba di Vittorio Emanuele II*. Marcia Funebre
MS band
    I:Tr (Ob. 48)

*XII Marce trionfali*
MS band
    I:Tr (Ob. 131)

## Senfl, ?

(3) *Trii*
MS 21-
    I:Ria (MS. 761)

(6) *Terzetti*
MS 21-
    I:Ria (MS. 759)

## Senofonte, Giovanni

(3) *Ordinanze per Trombe semplici* per l'Armata italiana
MS
    I:Tr (Ob. 63)

## Serra, Giovanni

*Marica* (composed to dedicate a new music school in 1856)
MS  Winds, accompanied by orchestra
    I:Gl (Sc.74)

## Serria, Giovanni (1787–1876)

*La Festa di S. Giovanni Marcia*
EP  (Milano, 1908)
    I:Mc (A.45.37.2)

*Santa Lutgarda.* Marcia Religiosa
EP  (Milano, 1908)
    I:Mc (A.45.37.3)

*Serenata*
EP  (Milano, 1908)
    I:Mc (A.45.37.4)

## Setti, Giacomo

*Marcia per Ottoni* in E♭
MS  8 winds
    I:REm (Mus.Sacra.V.15)

*Marcia funebre*
MS  band
    I:REm (Mus.Sacra.V.15 bis)

Nr. 8 *Marcie*
MS  21-122, piccolo, bass drun, organ
    I:REm (Mus.Sacra.V.2)

*Marcie e Adagi*
MS  1021-121, bombardone, bass drun
    I:REm (Mus.Sacra.V.4)

*Messe breve*
MS  TTB, winds, organ
    I:REm (Mus.Sacra.XI.25)

## Sighicelli, Vincenzo (1830–1892)

*Marcia trionfale*
MS  band
    I:Tr (Ob. 248)

## Smancini, ?

*Gran Valtzer*
MS  2011-
    I:OS (Ms.Mus.B.4843)

## Sparano, Giuseppe

*Marcia funebre*
EP  (Milano, 1897)
    I:Mc (A.45.37.14)

## Spontini, Gasparo Luigi (1774–1851)

*Fernando Cortez*
MS  222-12, contrabsn
    I:BGc (Mayr.E.2.12)

*Grosser Sieges- und Festmarsch*
EP  (Berlin, 1832)
    GB:Lbm (h.1509.o.[7.])
    US:DW

*Marche* in C
MS  13 part trumpets and trombones
    I:JESI:Camunale (Mus.Ms.Spont.-3)

*Preludio per Banda*. Ai combattenti e alla vittoria sul Campo di Marte
MS
    I:Mc (Noseda.R.19-37); US:DW (1135)
    This is a 28-page score for large band, 'Allegro Marziale.'

## Tadolini, Giovanni (1785–1872)

*Gran Quintetto*
MS  piano, 1101-01
    I:Bc

## Talini, Giuseppe

*Serenata con Var.*
MS   1001-11
    I:OS (Mss.Musische.B.4341)

## Tebaldini, Giovanni (1864–1952)

*Vexil1a*
MS TB chorus, brass band
I:PCd

## Tampia, Stefano (1832–1878)

The following compositions are all found in I:Tco.

*L'Autunno*
MS   female chorus, band

*Ave maris stella*, Op. 43 (1856)
MS   3 voices, band

*Il Canto*
MS   female chorus, band

*Come si ami la patria*
MS   voice and band

*Le Cri de l'Italie* (dedicated: Victor Emmanuel II)
MS   band

*La Frugalita*
MS   voice and band

*In Gabbia*
MS   voice and band

*Marcia originale*
MS   band

(3) *Marcia funebre* (Op. 42, 46, and 60)
MS   band

*Marcia trionfale*
MS   band

*Un'Ora mesta e un'ora lieta*
MS   solo, female chorus, band

*Palestro*. Gran marcia originale, Op. 63
MS  band

*La Parola*
MS  voice and band

*La Preghiera del mattino*
MS  voice and band

*La Preghiera della sera*
MS  voice and band

*Ringiazianento*
MS  voice and band

*La Rondinella*
MS  voice and band

*Stabat Mater*, Op. 40 (1856)
MS  3 voice choir and band

*Virginia*. Mazurka
MS  band

## Toschi, ?

*Pot-pourri, Un Ballo in Maschea* (Verdi)
MS  band
    I:FEM

## Tosoroni, ?

[an 1851 book on instrumentation]
EP
    I:Mc (Th.e.38)

## Trebbi, ?

*Rimembranza della tenebre*. Marcia
MS  band
    I:FEM

## Trento, Giuseppe

*Marcia Militaire* (1889)
MS  band
    I:Tr (Ob. 289)

*Polka brillante* (1889)
MS  band
    I:Tr (Ob. 290)

## Trombetti, ?

*Mazurca* (1864)
MS  band
    I:FEM

*Statuto*. Marcia (1868)
MS  band
    I:FEM

## Vaninetti, Giuseppe (b. 1849)

*Elegia* (for Umberto I)
EP  (Torino, 1900)
    I:Mc (A.45.38.29)

## Vecchi, G.

*Sestetto*
MS  1021-02
    I:OS (Ms.Mus.B.4403)

## Vessella, Alessandro (1860–1929)

Unless otherwise noted the following are original compositions, in score parts, found
    in I:Rasc.

*Elegia alla memoria di Goffredo Mameli*
MS  band

*Elegia alIa memoria di Vittorio Emanuele II*
MS  band

*AlIa Memoria di Vittorio Emanuelle II*, VIII Anniversario della sua morte
MS  band
    I:Tr (Ms. ob. 57)

*Overture in F minor alla manoria eli Vittorio Emanuelle II*, XII Anniversario della sua morte
MS  band
    I:Tr (Ms. (1). 328)

*Britannia* — Rapsodia
MS band
    I:Mc (A.45.43.17); also in I:Rasc

*Cairoli March*
MS band

*Campidoglio*
MS band

*Casamicciola Overture*
MS band

*Corteo Nuziale*
MS band

*Hurra nella venuta in Roma di S.M. Guglielmo II*
MS band

*In Memoria di Umberto I,* Marcia funebre
ED (?) band
    I:Mc (A.45.43.1)

*Inno dei Laneieri di Novara*
MS band

*Marcia del concorso*
MS band

*Marcia trionfale*
MS band

*Overture* in E♭
MS band

*II Overture* in E♭
MS band
    I:Rasc
    US:DW (1389)

*III Overture* in C
MS band
    I:Rasc
    US:DW (1390)

*IV Overture* in F minor
MS band
    I :Rasc
    US:DW (1145)

*Per la Festa degli Alberi-Canto*
MS band

*Ricordo del XX Settembre* — Fantasia
MS band

*Sinfonia* (1888)
MS 1222-02, contrabsn
    I:Fc (D.XI.2805)

*Fantasia sull'opera Fidelio* (Beethoven)
MS band

*Fantasia sull'opera Norma* (Bellini)
MS band

*1st & 2nd Divertimento sull'opera Carmen* (Bizet)
MS band
    I:Rasc
EP I:OS (Mss.Musiche B. 1913)

*Fantasia su 'Rintocco della rnezzanotte' di Carlini*
MS band

*Parafrasi dell'opera Gloria* di Cilea
MS band

*Reminiscenze dell'Histoire d'un Pierrot di Pasqule Costa*
MS band

*Fantasia sulla Lucrezia Borgia* (Donizetti)
MS band

*Fantasia sulla Aben Hamet di Dubois*
MS band

*Fantasia su La regata Nazionale di Elia*
MS band

*Fantasia sull'opera Il trillo del diavolo di Falchi*
MS band

*Fantasia sull'opera Faust* (Gounod)
MS band

*Fantasia sull'opera I Pagliacci* (Leoncavallo)
MS band

*Divertimento su L'Africana* (Meyerbeer)
MS band

*Fantasia su Il Perdono di Ploermal* (Meyerbeer)
MS band

*Fantasia su Gli Vgonotti* (Meyerbeer)
MS band

*Fantasia su Iris* (Mascagni)
MS band

*Impressioni dall'opera Isabeau* (Mascagni)
MS band

*Fantasia sull'opera I Rantzau* (Mascagni)
MS band

*Gran Fantasia sull'opera Il Cid* (Massenet)
MS band

*Fantasia sull'opera Il Re di Lahore* (Massenet)
MS band

*Fantasia sulla Francesca da Rimini* (Morlacchi)
MS band

*Fantasia su La Boheme* (Puccini)
MS band

*Fantasia sull'opera Manon Lescaut* (Puccini)
MS band

*Parafrasi della Tosca* (Puccini)
MS band

*Fantasia sull'opera Sansone e Dalila* (Saint-Saëns)
MS band

*Parafrasi di varie melodie di Tost*
MS band

*Fantasia sull'opera Aida* (Verdi)
MS band

*Grand Pot-pourri La Forza del Destino* (Verdi)
MS band

*Fantasia sull'opera Rigoletto* (Verdi)
MS band

*1st Preludio e Fantasia sull'opera Lohengrin* (Wagner)
MS  band

*Fantasia su Il Crepuscolo Degli Dei* (Wagner)
MS  band

*Fantasia su L'Oro del Reno* (Wagner)
MS  band

*Fantasia sull'opera Sigfrido* (Wagner)
MS  band

*Reminiscenze del I atto Tannhauser* (Wagner)
MS  band

*Fantasia sull'opera Tristano e Isotta* (Wagner)
MS  band

*Divertimento su Il Vascello Fantasma* (Wagner)
MS  band

*Fantasia su Il Vascello Fantasma* (Wagner)
MS  band
  I:Rasc (score & parts)

*Fantasia sull'opera Die Walkure* (Wagner)
MS  band

## Vincini, ?

*Napolitain pas redoublé*
EP  (London, 1877)
  GB:Lbm (f.412.h.[18.])

## Vitaliti, Sebastiano

*Sinfonia per Band. La Corona d'Italia* (for Umberto I)
MS  band
  I:Tr (ob.268)
  US:DW (1141)
  www.whitwellbooks.com

## Zanchi, Francesco

*Qui tollis*
MS  B, 20-121, st.bass, organ
  I:BGc (Mayr.53.38)

## Zandonati, Giovanni (1754–1838)

*Pastorale*
MS  organ, 12-22
    I:RVE [incomplete score]

## Zanti, Alessandro

*Serenata* (1812)
MS  21-02
    I:OS (Ms.Mus.B.4436) [cl. 1 and bassoon]
    I:OS (Ms.Mus.B.2967) [cl. 2]

## Zingarelli, Nicola (1752–1837)

*Sestetto*
MS  2022-
    I:Mc (Noseda R.23.8)

*Stabat mater* in D minor
MS  4 voices, 2-001, bass
    I:Nc (Mus.relig.4250)

## Zurlo, Giuseppe

*Fiori alpini Valtzer* (1896)
MS  band
    I:Tr (Ob. 63/2)

# Poland

**Elsner, Jozef (1769–1854)**

The following works, with wind accompaniment, are mentioned in William Smialek, *Jozef Elsner and Military Band Music in Nineteenth Century Poland.*

*Two Marches* for the National Guard (1831)

*Mass*, Op. 22 (1823)

*Te Deun*, Op. 39 (1825)

*Haec, requies mea*, Op. 43 (1827)
MS
      PL:Univ. Library, Krakow [Biblioteka Jagiellonska No. 1428 III]

*Hymn*, Op. 49 (1829)

*Requiem* , Op. 2
MS  SATB, 22-02, 2 basset horns

# Spain

**Matador, Jose**

*Spanish Valse*, 'Sevilla'
EP   (London, 1895)
    GB:Lbm (h.1549.)

# Turkey

**Simonich, Anna**

*The Pacha's Marsch*. Composed for the Turkish army by Her Excellency the wife of Omar Pacha. Adapted from the M.S. copy received by private means from the composer.

EP   (London, 1854)

    GB:Lbm (h.1324.[6.])

# The United States of America

## Laurendeau, L. P.

*Watch dis Chile*, Negro dance
EP   (Boston, IB96)
    GB:Lbm (f.800.[797.])

*Way down South*, Descriptive fantasia (with solo cornet)
EP   (Boston, I896)
    GB:Lbm (f.800.[798.])
    GB:Lbm has several other of his early prints from the early twentieth century.

## Luscomb, Fred

*On the War Path*, Galop
EP   (Boston, I898)
    GB:Lbm (f.800.[908.])

*Peruvian Dance* (with solo cornet)
EP   (New York, 1906)
    GB:Lbm (f.800.[909.])

## Metz, Theodore A.

*Give Cinda the Cake*, March and two-step
EP   (New York, I899)
    GB:Lbm (f.800.[964.])

## Morris, Sanuel

The following works were published in 1901 in Boston.

*Belles of America March*
    GB:Lbm (f.800.a.[9.])

*Legion of Honour*
    GB:Lbm (f.800.a.[10.])

*Love's Confession* (Characteristic piece)
    GB:Lbm (f.800.a.[11.])

*The Victorious Heroes March*
    GB:Lbm (f.800.a.[13.])

## Morton, Fdward

The following works were published in Boston in 1901.

*Emanuel*. Anthem, with solo cornet and chorus
GB:Lbm (f.800.a.[20.])

*English Songs*, with solo cornet
GB:Lbm (f.800.a.[21.])

*Lord of Lords*, Anthem, with solo cornet
GB:Lbm (f.800.a.[22.])

*Pretoria,* Fantasia, with solo cornet
GB:Lbm (f.800.a.[23.])

*Silchester*, Quick step (sacred), with solo cornet
GB:Lbm (f.800.a.[24.])

## Ramsdell, Eugene C.

*Comic Opera* in 1 act, 1 scene. Rehearsal of the Punkin Holler, gold plated, diamond tipped cornet band.
EP (Boston, 1900)
GB:Lbm (f.800.a.[131.])

*Soldiers of Uncle Sam March*
EP (Boston, 1900)
GB:Lbm (f.800.a.[132.])

## Rankine, T. B.

*Columbiana March*
EP (Boston, 1899)
GB:Lbm (f.800.a.[134.])

*The Gallant Rough Riders March*
EP (Boston, 1899)
GB:Lbm (f.800.a.[135.])

## Rayder, J. Henri

The following works were published, 1893–1896, in Boston.

*Break away*, Galop
GB:Lbm (f.800.a.[136.])

*Facilitation March*
    GB:Lbm (f.800.a.[137.])

*The Free Lance March*
    GB:Lbm (f.800.a.[138.])

*Hurry up,* Galop
    GB:Lbm (f.800.a.[140.])

*The Norseman March*
    GB:Lbm (f.800.a.[142.])

*Rustic Wedding Waltz*
    GB:Lbm (f.800.a.[143.])

*Sweet Remanbrance* Mazurka
    GB:Lbm (f.800.a.[144.])

## Reeves, D. W. (1838–1900)

*The Niagara* quick march
EP   (London, 1882)
    GB:Lbm (f.412.n.[13.])

## Rivers, Walter

*Duty's Call,* Quick march
EP   (Boston, 1901)
    GB:Lbm (f.800.a.[192.])

*The 'Standard,'* Quick march
EP   (London, Boston, 1901)
    GB:Lbm (f.800.a.[193.])

## Robinson, Alvan

*Massachusetts Collection of Martial Musick*, containing a plain, easy and concise introduction to the grounds of martial musick … together with a large collection of the most approved beats, marches, airs, & … Designed principally for the benefit of the militia of the United States.
EP   (New Hampshire, 1820)
    GB:Lbm (a.226.d.)

## Rockwell, Charles J.

The following works were published, 1901–1903, in Boston.

*Across the Pacific March*
    GB:Lbm (f.800.a.[205.])

*Fires of Glory*, Overture
    GB:Lbm (f.800.a.[206.])

*Ninth U.S. Infantry March*
    GB:Lbm (f.800.a.[207.])

*Post of Danger March*
    GB:Lbm (f.800.a.[208.])

*Ramona Waltz*
    GB:Lbm (f.800.a.[209.])

## Rollinson, T. H. (1844–1928)

The following works were published, 1893–1904, in Boston.

*Aladdin Overture*
    GB:Lbm (f.800.a.[221.])

*Brunette and Blonde*, Concert polka (with solo or soli cornets)
    GB:Lbm (f.800.a.[223.])

*By Moonlight*, Serenade
    GB:Lbm (f.800.a.[224.])

*Castles in the Air*, Waltz
    GB:Lbm (f.800.a.[226.])

*The Cavalier*, Overture
    GB:Lbm (f.800.a.[228.])

*Cherry ripe*, Mazurka
    GB:Lbm (f.800.a.[229.])

*Chula Vista March*
    GB:Lbm (f.800.a.[230.])

*Gallant Hearts March*
    GB:Lbm (f.800.a.[237.])

*Guard of Honor March*
    GB:Lbm (f.800.a.[241.])

*Heroic March*
GB:Lbm (f.800.a.[242.])

*The Hub March*
GB:Lbm (f.800.a.[243.])

*The Hunting of the Snark*, An epical prody in six cantos
GB:Lbm (f.800.a.[244.])

*The Ice King March*
GB:Lbm (f.800.a.[245.])

*Idle Moments*, Entr'acte
GB:Lbm (f.800.a.[246.])

*Ildica Waltz*
GB:Lbm (f.800.a.[247.])

*Jollification March*
GB:Lbm (f.800.a.[250.])

*The Jolly Millers*, galop
GB:Lbm (f.800.a.[251.])

*King of the Track* galop
GB:Lbm (f.800.a.[253.])

*A Little Bit of 'Essence,'* a two step oddity
GB:Lbm (f.800.a.[254.])

*Love's Missive Waltz*
GB:Lbm (f.800.a.[255.])

*March–Polonaise*
GB:Lbm (f.800.a.[257.])

*Merry Wedding Bells*, Schottisch
GB:Lbm (f.800.a.[258.])

*Meteoric March*
GB:Lbm (f.800.a.[259.])

*Moonlight Fancies Waltz*
GB:Lbm (f.800.a.[260.])

*Morning Breezes Waltz*
GB:Lbm (f.800.a.[261.])

*A Morning in Noah's Ark*, Humorous phantasy in four scenes
GB:Lbm (f.800.a.[263.])

*The Naiad Queen*, Cverture (with piano)
GB:Lbm (h.3673.[27.])

*Nydia Waltz*
GB:Lbm (f.800.a.[264.])

*Nynph and Satyr*
GB:Lbm (f.800.a.[265.])

*The Old oaken Bucket March*
GB:Lbm (f.800.a.[266.])

*Ole Virginny Days*, two step
GB:Lbm (f.800.a.[267.])

*The Overland Limited Galop*
GB:Lbm (f.800.a.[268.])

*The Quill Section March*
GB:Lbm (f.800.a.[269.])

*Red as a Rose Polka*
GB:Lbm (f.800.a.[271.])

*Souvenir of Otay March*
GB:Lbm (f.800.a.[272.])

*Tu-Whit Polka*
GB:Lbm (f.800.a.[275.])

*Twilight Shadows Waltz*
GB:Lbm (f.800.a.[276.])

*Uncle Rufe's Jubilee* two step
GB:Lbm (f.800.a.[278.])

*Village Bells*, Characteristic piece
GB:Lbm (f.800.a.[279.])

*The Whirling Dervishes*, A desert episode
GB:Lbm (f.800.a.[280.])

*With merry Hearts Waltz*
GB:Lbm (f.800.a.[283.])

## Sousa, John Philip (1854–1932)

*The Directorate March*
EP   (Cincinnati, 1894)
    GB:Lbm (f.800.a.[361.])

# Index

# Index of Names

## A

Abbati, ?, 19th century Italian composer for band, 172

Abbiati, Dionigio, 19th century Italian composer for band, 172

Abdul-Meyjd, Sultan of Turkey, 198, 244

Aber, Giovanni, late 18th century Italian composer, *Sonata* for six winds, 33

Abert, Johann, 1832–1915, German composer of church music with brass, 96

Abt, composer included in a 1874 English collection of band music, 113

Acerbi, Domenico, 1842–1921, Italian composer for band, 172

Ackermann, composer 19th century English band collections, 116ff

Adams, Stephen, 1841–1913, pseud. For Michael Maybrick, English composer, 118

Adler, ?, late 18th century Italian composer, 34

Agnola, Giacomo, 1761–1845, Italian composer for band, 172

Agostinelli, ?, 19th century Italian composer, concerti for 3 flutes, 173

Albanese, Luigi, b. 1859, Italian composer; church work for chorus & band, 173

Albert, Charles, 1864–1932, German composer, 96

Albinoni, Tommaso, 1671–1750, Italian composer of Hautboisten; oboe music, 13

Alcampo, Matteo, 19th century Italian composer for band, 173

Alessandro, Michele, 1859–1918, Italian composer, *Elegy for Umberto I* for band, 173

Aliani, Nicola, 19th century Italian composer; church work voices & winds, 173

Aloe, Luigi, b. 1829, Italian composer for band, 173

Altafulla, Ubaldo, fl. 1800–1810, Italian composer, 34

Andolfi, Guglielmo, 1847–1928, Italian composer for band, 173

André, 18th century publisher in Offenbach, 18, 100

Androet, Cesare, 1827–1889, 174

Anna-Vanni, Giuseppe, 19th century Italian composer, *Sinfonia* for band, 174

Annoscia, Enrico, 19th century Italian composer, 174

Arban, J. J., 1825–1889, French composer of works for band, 65

Arbuckle, composer included in a 1887 English collection of band music, 116

Arezzo Della Targia, Giambattista, 19th century Italian composer, 174

Aria, Giuseppe, 19th century Italian composer for band, 174

Arici, Marco, 1778–1827, Italian composer, 34

Asch, Georg, 19th century English composer for band, 118

Ascolese, Raffele, 1855–1923, Italian composer for band, 174

Asioli, Bonifazio, 1769–1832, Italian composer for band, 175

Asioli, Raffaele, 1817–1899, Italian composer, 175

Auber, unidentified work arranged by Lindpainter, 105

Auberlen, Louis, 19th century German composer, 95

Audran, ?, composer included in 19th century English band collections, 115, 116

Avalione, Vincenzo, 19th century Italian composer, *Sinfonia* (1878) for band, 175

Avoni, Petronio, b. 1790, arranger of unidentified works by Cimaroso and Paisiello, 175

Avseri de Chistofano, Giuseppe, 19th century Italian composer for band, 175

## B

Baccherini, Francesco, 19th century Italian composer for band, 175

Bach, J. S., 1685–1750, German composer, 5

Bado, Giuseppe, 19th century Italian composer for Harmoniemusik, 176

Baier, composer included in a 1875 English collection of band music, 114

Baioni, Massimo, 19th century Italian composer for band, 176

Banchi, Giuseppe, 19th century Italian composer for band, 176

Baragatti, Romeo, 19th century Italian composer, 176

Barberis, Pier, 19th century Italian composer, funeral music for Ponchielli for band, 176

Bärmann, Heinrich, 1784–1847, German composer of a clarinet work with band, 96

Barreca, D., 19th century Italian orchestrator, 205

Bartolomeas, composer included in a 1875 English collection of band music, 114

Bartolucci, Mariano, 19th century Italian composer, overture for band, 176

Baryzehnikoff, composer included in a 1871 English collection of band music, 113

Baschieri, Giovanni, 19th century Italian composer for band, 176

Batley, Thomas, composer included in a 1893 English collection of band music, 116

Battaglia, Giacinto, 1803–1861, 19th century Italian composer, 177

Bausteder, ?, German Baroque composer, 5

# About the Author

Dr. David Whitwell is a graduate ('with distinction') of the University of Michigan and the Catholic University of America, Washington DC (PhD, Musicology, Distinguished Alumni Award, 2000) and has studied conducting with Eugene Ormandy and at the Akademie für Musik, Vienna. Prior to coming to Northridge, Dr. Whitwell participated in concerts throughout the United States and Asia as Associate First Horn in the USAF Band and Orchestra in Washington DC, and in recitals throughout South America in cooperation with the United States State Department.

At the California State University, Northridge, which is in Los Angeles, Dr. Whitwell developed the CSUN Wind Ensemble into an ensemble of international reputation, with international tours to Europe in 1981 and 1989 and to Japan in 1984. The CSUN Wind Ensemble has made professional studio recordings for BBC (London), the Köln Westdeutscher Rundfunk (Germany), NOS National Radio (The Netherlands), Zürich Radio (Switzerland), the Television Broadcasting System (Japan) as well as for the United States State Department for broadcast on its 'Voice of America' program. The CSUN Wind Ensemble's recording with the Mirecourt Trio in 1982 was named the 'Record of the Year' by The Village Voice. Composers who have guest conducted Whitwell's ensembles include Aaron Copland, Ernest Krenek, Alan Hovhaness, Morton Gould, Karel Husa, Frank Erickson and Vaclav Nelhybel.

Dr. Whitwell has been a guest professor in 100 different universities and conservatories throughout the United States and in 23 foreign countries (most recently in China, in an elite school housed in the Forbidden City). Guest conducting experiences have included the Philadelphia Orchestra, Seattle Symphony Orchestra, the Czech Radio Orchestras of Brno and Bratislava, The National Youth Orchestra of Israel, as well as resident wind ensembles in Russia, Israel, Austria, Switzerland, Germany, England, Wales, The Netherlands, Portugal, Peru, Korea, Japan, Taiwan, Canada and the United States.

He is a past president of the College Band Directors National Association, a member of the Prasidium of the International Society for the Promotion of Band Music, and was a member of the founding board of directors of the World Association for Symphonic Bands and Ensembles (WASBE). In 1964 he was made an honorary life member of Kappa Kappa Psi, a national professional music fraternity. In September, 2001, he was a delegate to the UNESCO Conference on Global Music in Tokyo. He has been knighted by sovereign organizations in France, Portugal and Scotland and has been awarded the gold medal of Kerkrade, The Netherlands, and the silver medal of Wangen, Germany, the highest honor given wind conductors in the United States, the medal of the Academy of Wind and Percussion Arts (National Band Association) and the highest honor given wind conductors in Austria, the gold medal of the Austrian Band Association. He is a member of the Hall of Fame of the California Music Educators Association.

Dr. Whitwell's publications include more than 127 articles on wind literature including publications in Music and Letters (London), the London Musical Times, the Mozart-Jahrbuch (Salzburg), and 39 books, among which is his 13-volume *History and Literature of the Wind Band and Wind Ensemble* and an 8-volume series on *Aesthetics in Music*. In addition to numerous modern editions of early wind band music his original compositions include 5 symphonies.

David Whitwell was named as one of six men who have determined the course of American bands during the second half of the 20th century, in the definitive history, *The Twentieth Century American Wind Band* (Meredith Music).

A doctoral dissertation by German Gonzales (2007, Arizona State University) is dedicated to the life and conducting career of David Whitwell through the year 1977. David Whitwell is one of nine men described by Paula A. Crider in *The Conductor's Legacy* (Chicago: GIA, 2010) as 'the legendary conductors' of the 20th century.

'I can't imagine the 2nd half of the 20th century—without David Whitwell and what he has given to all of the rest of us.' Frederick Fennell (1993)

www.ingramcontent.com/pod-product-compliance
Lightning Source LLC
Chambersburg PA
CBHW080414270326
41929CB00018B/3016